Marriage Toners

Marriage Toners

Weekly Exercises to Strengthen Your Relationship

Larry and Rebecca Jordan

Fleming H. Revell
A Division of Baker Book House Co
Grand Rapids, Michigan 49516

Published by Fleming H. Revell
a division of Baker Book House Company
P.O. Box 6287, Grand Rapids, MI 49516-6287

Printed in the United States of America

Library of Congress Cataloging-in-Publication Data

Jordan, Larry.
    Marriage toners : Weekly exercises to strengthen your relationship / Larry and Rebecca Jordan.
        p.   cm.
    Includes bibliographical references (p.).
    ISBN 0-8007-5562-6
    1. Married people—Prayer-books and devotions—English. 2. Marriage—Religious aspects—Christianity. I. Jordan, Rebecca. II. Title.
BV4596.M3J67   1995
248.8′4—dc20   95-1467

To our daughters, Valerie and Jennifer,
for their unconditional love and support

∽ Contents ∽

∾ *Acknowledgments* ∾

Thanks go to our friends, Drs. Brian and Deborah Newman, for introducing us to marriage enrichment leadership training; to each of the couples who have shared their personal marriage experiences with us in the book; and to all who have been a part of our marriage enrichment retreats, as well as the many friends and coworkers from our church who have encouraged us, prayed for us, and even provided a quiet place for us to work during this project.

We appreciate Lois and Dixon Murrah for their support and encouragement to us and other couples in ministry.

Special thanks go to our literary agent, Helen K. Hosier, whose friendship, work, and encouragement have helped make this book possible.

We would also like to thank William Petersen and the editorial staff at Baker Book House.

And finally, special words of gratitude to our parents for their love and support through the years, and to our daughters, Valerie and Jennifer, who never stop believing in us.

❧ *Preface* ❧

No matter how good a marriage appears, it can always improve. Habits and routine dull the relationship, and from time to time we need to take an honest look at where we are.

We believe communication is a key to brightening marriages. If you're willing to talk honestly and openly together, with Christ as the center of your life, you can work through any marriage issue. The mutual understanding you gain in the process will deepen the joys of intimacy.

In this book you'll find seven categories of exercises for couples. They cover every topic from romance to retirement. Choose any subject you want to work on together, but we suggest you begin with fun, nonthreatening issues at first.

Take all the time you need. You can do one exercise each week, or you may want to spend several weeks on just one topic. It may take longer to work through some goals than others. You may want to come back and redo exercises to see how your relationship has grown. Work through the book in the way that's best for you, as a couple. You might consider getting two copies of the book so each of you can have a personal workbook. This lifetime marriage enrichment guide is designed not to replace but to enhance marriage enrichment group events, counseling, or personal in-depth therapy.

Setting goals—and accomplishing them—takes commitment. But isn't that what love really is—commitment? Make your goals practical, as well as specific. For example, one goal for "Special Dates" might be to plan a night out once or twice a month at a new restaurant—just for the two of you. Review your goals often. Keep them visible as constant reminders.

For fifteen years our marriage was "unconscious." We went through the motions with little emotional intimacy. Since that time we have learned what it means to really work at marriage. With God's help, we committed ourselves to goal-setting exercises, ones like you'll find in this book. Today, after almost thirty years of marriage, a deep commitment to each other and a desire to honor Jesus Christ through our marriage keep us focused and eager to grow in oneness together.

Not long ago, a single young woman bought a cocker spaniel puppy from us. Unfortunately, I (Becky) had already become attached to it. When I watched that sweet puppy walk out of our lives, I couldn't hold back the tears. Can you believe that? As we watched them go, Larry reached over and gave me a tender reassuring hug—nothing unusual.

The young lady brought the dog back the next day. Her landlord refused to allow it into the apartment complex. Before she left she said, "Someday, I want a marriage like yours."

"What do you mean?" I asked, puzzled by her statement.

"You know, the way your husband hugged you when I left yesterday. I could tell you love each other by the look in your eyes."

It was a simple observation, but we got the message. People are watching our marriages to see if the light's really on. Before that young lady left, we had the privilege of introducing her to the only Light we know.

One current author believes a marriage should be whatever the partners want it to be, even if it means leading separate lives, having separate interests, and occupying separate bedrooms. Our prayer is that this book will help you make your marriage what *God* wants it to be. Then your marriage will be a testimony, a light shining brightly—like a city on a hilltop—honoring him.

You are the light of the world. A city on a hill cannot be hidden. Neither do people light a lamp and put it under a bowl. Instead they put it on its stand, and it gives light to everyone in the house. In the same way, let your light [marriage] shine before men, that they may see your good deeds and praise your Father in heaven.

Matthew 5:14–16

Let our lives and our love
Show the world why Jesus came,
Let them know,
His love has made us one.

Chris Machen
Commitment Song

Renewing Romance Exercises

Romance

Roses, cards, love's true art
A quiet, living-room dance;
Prepare the place, embrace my heart—
Lead me to romance.

The Exercise Goal

To add the excitement of romance to our marriage.

The Biblical Idea

The Old Testament book Song of Songs not only gives an allegory of Christ and his love for the church—his bride on earth—but also unveils a beautiful portrait of romantic love between a husband and wife.

Scattered throughout this unusual book of the Bible are word pictures of spoken expectations, secret longings, romantic desires, and sexual love. In the Song of Songs we smell the fragrance of sweet perfume and see the bride arrayed in her most feminine lingerie. We sense the warm touch of gentle hands and feel the excitement of passionate lovemaking. And if we listen carefully, we hear the whispers of a sensitive groom preparing his bride for a romantic rendezvous and the affectionate words of a bride affirming her beloved husband. Here is romance with a capital R.

The Need

With all the books available now on the differences between men and women, it's amazing the number of couples we counsel who are still clueless as to the need for romance in marriage. Most women need and love all the trappings of romance: flowers, tender words, candlelight, thoughtful gifts, special dates. These pave the road to spontaneity, warmth, and responsiveness in women.

For some men, it may be a little different. Larry admits that in the past, romance was not on his personal priority list. As he began to understand my need, however, he intentionally created that atmosphere for me. In the process, he developed a taste for romance as well.

One night Larry turned our loft into a beautiful garden, complete with plants from all over the house, soft lights and music, chilled juice, and our own romantic picnic—all without leaving the house. When I travel, Larry usually meets me at the airport with fresh roses. He holds my hand in public, opens car doors, and loves to arrange romantic getaways, because those are the things I like.

When Larry was away on an overseas mission trip, he opened his suitcase and found two weeks' worth of "I love you" cards I had prepared for him, one to open each night while we were apart.

Romance is the appetizer before the main meal. It's the loving mood you create with your spouse all day, all month, all year. Men, remember: The way to a woman's heart is through romance.

The Exercise

What spells romance to you? An overnight getaway? Friday night at the movies? Holding hands in public? Soft music and candlelight? Each of you should write answers to the following.

1. Three things I think of when I hear the word romance.

2. Three romantic things we've (you've) done in the past that I like.

3. Three romantic things I'd like us (you) to do in the future.

The Plan

Spend some time together discussing and clarifying the answers you both wrote above. These answers should give you ideas for how to add romance to your marriage. Decide on three specific things you can do together to reach that goal. For each one, be sure to make decisions about details such as time and place. If your plan isn't specific, you won't be able to reach your goal. Write your final plans below.

1.

2.

3.

∽ 2 ∽
Special Dates

"You don't bring me flowers anymore!"
"You cook me TV dinners from the store!"
It's not too late. Let's plan a date—
What are we waiting for?

The Exercise Goal

To show love to my mate by planning special dates together.

The Biblical Idea

"I don't love you anymore." Like an unexpected gun blast, those words shock and frighten any mate. In Revelation 2, that's exactly the charge God levels at the church in Ephesus: They don't love him anymore. This picture pulls at your heartstrings. The church, the bride of Christ, has left its first love.

"Go back to the beginning," God says (our paraphrase). "Change, and do the things you once did when the fires of your love first burned brightly."

Can we not apply the same truth to marriage? Has your love waned through the years? Have you left your first love? Go back to the beginning. Renew your vows. It's never too late to start over.

The Need

One of the best ways to rekindle a dying flame in marriage is to use the same fuel that first sparked it. Think about your dating years. Visualize youthful energies and young love—you know, the times you couldn't wait to see each other again. Go back to the days when you spent hours thinking up special things to do together. (Has it been that long?)

Dating doesn't have to end after the honeymoon. A marriage continues to sizzle when its partners get serious about fanning the flames.

16

Whether it's as simple as escaping to a Friday night dinner date or as exotic as kidnapping your spouse for a surprise trip to a mountain hideaway, make time to spend together. If Grandma lives too far away to keep the kids, budget money for child care or join a baby-sitting pool with friends.

Talk about what you like to do. Take turns planning dates. And if you need help with creativity, check out your local bookstore for books suggesting fresh dating ideas. You'll find everything from helicopter rides and midnight swims to stay-at-home game nights and garage sale bargain hunts.

Planning special dates may require research. We know one young couple who are masters at digging for new dating ideas. The husband is constantly asking friends about new places to try, getting all the necessary information and then planning out the details of a fresh dating experience.

Larry keeps a file of new restaurants and places to go, as well as a running list of my "I'd-like-to-try-that-sometime" comments.

Kris and Al's busy lifestyle is a challenge that requires extra creativity for special dates together. One of their favorite "cheap dates" is what they call a "Penny Drive." They start out in the car together and flip a penny at each corner to determine their destination. Heads, go right. Tails, go left. They drive until they run out of turns or it's time to go home. This date gives them time to get away and talk plus discover some unusual back roads.

We guarantee, as do the couples in our marriage enrichment groups, that nothing keeps the flame burning brighter than planning special times together you both enjoy. If you really love each other, care enough to keep dating.

The Exercise

Think about the times you spent together before you married. Where did you go? What did you enjoy doing together? Can you recreate some elements of those past dating experiences? Complete these exercises and share your answers together.

1. Three special dates I remember before we married.

2. Three kinds of dates we've had recently that I've enjoyed and would like to repeat.

3. Three special dates we've never tried but I would like to plan in the future.

The Plan

Discuss and clarify your answers above. Then make a plan to reach your goal of having special dates together. You should decide how often you will have a date, how to pay for it, what to do with the children, as well as what you will do and who will make the arrangements.

How often?

How will we pay for it?

Who will care for the children?

Date idea #1_____

　　　When? _____

　　　Who will arrange? _____

Date idea #2_____

　　　When? _____

　　　Who will arrange? _____

Date idea #3_____

　　　When? _____

　　　Who will arrange? _____

Gifts

I own enough appliances!
My socks are not too few!
If you really want to please me,
Then give the gift of you.

The Exercise Goal

To discover gifts that bring joy and pleasure to my mate.

The Biblical Idea

There's more to a gift than you may think. A rose is not just a rose, and a diamond may be more than a girl's best friend. The gifts the magi brought to Jesus at his birth weren't just gold, frankincense, and myrrh. These offerings symbolized their love and affection for the long-awaited Messiah. Their gifts represented a long journey, made just so they could worship this holy child.

Nothing we could give to God, to others, or to our mates could compare to the love gift God gave to us through his son Jesus. But we can give with the same attitude—from a heart of love, unselfishly and unreservedly.

The Need

The gifts you select for your husband or wife are also symbols. They reflect how well you listen and how unselfish and intentional you are in selecting a gift your mate would really like.

When I (Larry) graduated from college, I went straight to graduate school and there was no money to buy a college ring. On a recent birthday, twenty-five years after my graduation, Becky surprised me with my college ring. I loved it!

Giving gifts that please is not all that difficult. Examine your motive. Are you buying this because you like it, or is this something you know your spouse would choose? Stay away from gifts you think your mate needs. Jesus needed nothing but swaddling clothes when he was born. The gifts the magi brought were lavish expressions of love, not responses to a need.

Try these guidelines for help in buying gifts that please:

1. Keep a running list of things you hear your mate say he or she would like.
2. Watch for styles and colors he or she wears often.
3. Husbands, don't buy your wife a gift that plugs in unless she asks for it.
4. Wives, eliminate socks from your gift list. Buy him those during the year, not for Christmas or birthdays.
5. Save up for that item you know your mate always wanted but never could afford.

The Exercise

Work through the following exercises on your own. Then share your responses together, making notes on your mate's likes and dislikes. Use this information to set goals on how you can make your gift-giving experiences in the future a joy and delight for your mate.

1. A favorite gift my mate gave me in the past.

2. Gifts I would like to receive in the future.

3. Gifts I'd rather not receive.

The Plan

Discuss the answers you both gave above. Write below three ways you will use to discover what gifts will bring joy to your mate.

1.

   2.

   3.

   Write below three gifts you will try to give to your mate, based on your discussion.

   1.

   2.

   3.

∞ 4 ∞
Places to Go

The opera? play? a movie?
Out to eat again?
No McDonald's, please. Let's go
A place we've never been.

The Exercise Goal

To add variety to our marriage by finding new places to go together.

The Biblical Idea

Do you remember the children's song, "Be Careful Little Eyes"? It was probably based on Colossians 3:17: "And whatever you do, whether in word or deed, do it all in the name of the Lord Jesus, giving thanks to God. . . ." Whatever you see, whatever you do, whatever you hear, wherever you go—the only guideline is to make sure it honors and glorifies God.

The Need

Are you tired of McDonald's? Have you seen *Jurassic Park* ten times? Is your leisure time totally predictable? How do you break out of the rut?

We'll probably keep harping on variety in married life, but only because it's so important. Determining new places to go requires planning. And if you plan together, the anticipation is as much fun as the going.

No money? No problem! How about a few hours browsing in the library or feeding the ducks at a nearby lake? We're thankful for friends who have offered us their vacation homes for a few days: a cabin by the lake, a trailer parked in a quiet, green meadow, or a spare bedroom in the Colorado mountains.

When the budget is tight, try an "I wish" shopping trip—just for the fun of it. In one of the more exclusive department stores, Becky gave me a private fashion show, modeling designer dresses and swimsuits.

Been to the zoo lately? A concert? A new restaurant? Be creative. One of Kris and Al's favorite pastimes is scouting out pawn shops. They once found a nine-hundred-dollar racing bike for sixty-five dollars. Gina and John, a couple still enjoying the exuberance of young adulthood, like to go to the drag races once a year. Find what smokes your tires and go for it!

The Exercise

List some places where you'd like to go. One part of your list could include vacation spots; another, special daytime or evening outings. Share your lists with each other; then compare them.

1. Circle the places you both mentioned and place a star beside them.

2. Divide the others into His and Hers columns.

3. Each week or month alternately choose a place from these lists you both like and a place only one of you suggests, taking turns between His and Hers columns. If either of you dislikes a place, strive for a compromise—two places in the same day, one each of you enjoys.

4. You also may want to list three places where you have no desire to go.

The Plan

Based on your discussion of the items above, choose three new places to go together. Decide when you will go.

1. Where we will go _____

   When we will go _____

2. Where we will go _____

   When we will go _____

3. Where we will go _____

   When we will go _____

∞ 5 ∞
Love in Action

If you really want to show me
That your love is here to stay,
Prove it in the little things
You do for me each day.

The Exercise Goal

To develop ways of expressing genuine love to my mate.

The Biblical Idea

Love notes tucked away in a lunch box, special messages that say, "You're awesome!", constant support even through the tough times—these and other affirmations of love paint a practical picture of 1 Corinthians 13, a passage that illustrates the kind of love we want and need from our mates.

"Follow the way of love," says 1 Corinthians 14:1. And what is that way? Perhaps Jesus would describe it as the narrow road, a journey of selfless giving, a way of mutual celebrations—a road not traveled by most. "I love you" means nothing from the mouth of one who refuses to demonstrate that love. "Let us not love with words or tongue but with actions and in truth," 1 John 3:18 says. Christlike love doesn't flinch when a husband loses his job. Christlike love doesn't throw in the towel on the grounds of incompatibility. Christlike love "bears all things, believes all things, hopes all things."

The Need

Soon after they say "I do," couples often change their theme song from "Love Makes the World Go 'Round" to "You Don't Bring Me Flowers Anymore." Whether we've been married two years or fifty-two years, each of us has the need to be loved and to feel secure. One benefit of continued affirmations of love is that they help create that sense of security between a husband and wife.

When Larry and I were going through a difficult period in our marriage, fears surfaced for the first time. I was reluctant to share my opinions for fear I would rock our marital boat. My patterns of "Yes, Larry" and "Whatever you say, Larry" only sent my resentment underground. I didn't feel safe to challenge him with, "I disagree," or to suggest, "Have you thought about this?"

A counselor friend challenged us to give each other "love affirmations" several times a week to help us create an atmosphere of security in which we could work through our conflicts. We each listed special acts of love we would like the other person to do for us. We wrote requests such as, "I would like you to fix a big breakfast once a week" or "I would like for you to rub my back before bedtime." We avoided controversial issues. We also gave each other the freedom to say, "I'd rather not do that right now." Some affirmations were things we practiced while dating but had stopped after marriage.

At first we felt selfish about asking for those things but soon found a real joy both in giving and receiving loving acts. Two positive results followed. First, the actions created a sense of security between us, enabling us to communicate negative feelings without fear of rejection from each other. Second, when we gave a loving act, we found that we enjoyed giving it as much as receiving it.

We are not saying you should live to please your mate. There's a difference between living only to please your partner (codependency) and giving pleasure. Living to please is like giving a balloon to someone but holding on to the string. Some of the motive is selfish. Truly giving pleasure, just for the sake of giving, always turns the string loose. It is selfless.

The Exercise

Complete the following exercises and share them together.

1. What do you consider to be a loving behavior? Discuss.

2. Three love affirmations I like that you're doing for me now.

3. Three love affirmations I liked that you gave me in the past.

4. Make a list of positive love affirmations you'd like for your mate to give or do for you, as long or short a list as you wish. Then exchange lists and agree to choose at least one affirmation to give each other daily.

The Plan

Discuss a long-term plan for using concrete ways to express your love for your spouse. Set three dates to make new lists of love affirmations and to review the old ones.

1.

2.

3.

∽ 6 ∽
Surprises

Though routine is great and plans are nice
For getting everything done,
They leave us in a marriage rut.
Surprises add some fun!

The Exercise Goal

To keep our marriage fresh and spontaneous.

The Biblical Idea

Jesus loved to surprise others—turning water to wine at a wedding feast, feeding over five thousand people with five loaves of bread and two fishes, interrupting funeral processions to raise the dead, and what about all his appearing and disappearing after his resurrection? These were not your ordinary, run-of-the-mill events. No one could accuse Jesus of being dull or predictable!

The Need

Larry jokes about not liking surprises, and I hint about wanting some more. It isn't that he dislikes having special things done for him, he just wants to know what to expect and when to expect it. But practical as he is, Larry truly loves to be surprised in small ways—with his favorite meal, a thoughtful gift, or a special evening of spontaneous romance. The surprises I like are different—I love a trip away, a treasured gift, or flowers anytime.

A few years ago, Larry caught a ten-pound bass on a private lake. He released the fish, but two years later I had an exact reproduction of it made from a picture and had it mounted for him. Ever seen a grown man kiss a fish? He was elated!

Recently I surprised Larry by arranging an all-day fishing trip for him on his favorite bass lake with a professional guide. Maybe I'm finally learning to speak his language. He's beginning to really love those surprises!

Try surprising your mate with progressive gifts, as does one couple we know. Throughout a special evening, they'll surprise each other with several gifts at different times just to prolong the suspense.

Does making a list of surprises ruin the spontaneity? No, because you still don't know when you'll get one. And you can always copy Larry's method. He listens when I comment about something I like, records it in a notebook, and then gives me that gift on a special occasion. One year in our women's ministry fashion show, I modeled a red, hand-quilted jumper. I fell in love with it but knew we couldn't afford it. Guess what Larry gave me the next Christmas?

Give a surprise for a special occasion, or for no reason at all, but it should fit these guidelines:

- It should be unexpected.
- It should be something your mate will enjoy.
- It should cost you something: time, money, or energy.
- It should be given in love.

A surprise, like a random act of kindness, softens the heart and keeps the relationship exciting. If you must compete in your marriage, compete by seeing who can outdo loving the other. Love loves to surprise!

The Exercise

Complete the exercises below alone. Then exchange your list with your partner, and tuck it away for future use. As you do these exercises, remember that surprises may or may not require money. They are unique to you and your mate.

1. A surprise (or surprises) my mate gave me in the past that I liked.

2. Kinds of surprises I don't like.

3. Surprises I'd like to receive from my mate. These may be places to go, things to do, or special gifts requiring either time or money.

The Plan

To help your marriage be fresh, plan three surprises for your mate and write down when you'll do them. Keep this list to yourself!

1. Surprise _____

   Date I'll do it _____

2. Surprise _____

   Date I'll do it _____

3. Surprise _____

   Date I'll do it _____

∾ 7 ∾
Sexuality

At times I feel as warm as toast
And sometimes, more like ice.
Together, can we work it out
And find out all the whys.

The Exercise Goal

To achieve greater sexual intimacy by understanding my mate's background and ideas of sexuality.

The Biblical Idea

After describing the qualities of godly wives, Peter then addresses husbands. "Be considerate as you live with your wives, and treat them with respect" (1 Peter 3:7). In other words, be patient and spend time getting to know what makes your wife tick! Proverbs 16:22 says, "Understanding is a fountain of life to those who have it." Understanding is the source of life, the key to growth, a river of enjoyment to those who work at it. And where else in marriage but in sexuality do we need more knowledge and understanding to achieve greater intimacy? First Corinthians 7 further challenges couples to treat one another's bodies with respect and love, giving to each other completely, neither withholding nor demanding, loving one another as they do their own bodies.

The Need

In a world where anything goes and nothing is hidden, couples may become confused about their own sexuality. Problems may arise if they perceived inaccurate sexual messages in childhood or adolescence. Pornography, sexual abuse, or parental absence in childhood or adolescence can later affect a couple's relationship negatively. Prob-

31

lems occur when people distort sex from God's original plan laid out in Genesis 2.

On the other hand, couples who grew up in homes where their parents viewed the sexual relationship as a natural, God-given celebration will need far less adjustment as adults.

Openness about sexual ideas and backgrounds, as well as an understanding of each other's differences as male and female, will help collapse most of the sexual barriers couples encounter. Good communication and understanding are crucial to sexual intimacy.

The Exercise

Let your answers be springboards of communication to help your mate understand you better.

1. Three words that describe my family of origin's attitudes about sexuality.

2. Any experiences that may have contributed to my current view of sexuality.

3. My views of sexuality as a child and teen.

4. Three differences I see in the way we approach our sexuality.

5. Three positive words that describe how I feel about our sexuality.

The Plan

After discussing your mate's background and ideas of sexuality, list three ways your understanding can lead to greater intimacy. Include any problems and ideas for solving them.

1.
2.
3.

∞ *8* ∞
Lovemaking

From the first good morning kiss
To the final night's embrace,
Let's talk of love—prepare my mind,
And I'll prepare the place.

The Exercise Goal

To enjoy lovemaking as a God-given gift.

The Biblical Idea

"Rejoice in the wife of your youth. . . . Let her breasts satisfy you at all times; be exhilarated always with her love" (Prov. 5:18–19 NASB). No room for boring lovemaking here! The Hebrew word for *exhilarated* paints a picture of a husband and wife intoxicated with their sexual union. Here is a couple drunk on love!

Song of Songs portrays lovemaking as a beautiful, exciting, and mutually satisfying experience for marriage partners. The dialogue between Solomon and his bride, Shulamith, reflects visual, sensory, and auditory pleasures: "Your eyes. . . . are doves. . . . Your lips are like a scarlet ribbon. . . . Your two breasts are like two fawns" (Song of Songs 4:1, 3, 5).

They communicate well their likes and their expectations: "Let my lover come into his garden and taste its choice fruits" (Song of Songs 4:16). They seem to enjoy the anticipation of their lovemaking as much as the act itself. True, these were newlyweds, but the words we cited earlier from Proverbs speak to couples of all ages. It's almost as if God is saying, "Sex is good. Sex is fun. Sex is my gift in marriage to you. Enjoy!"

The Need

Sexual intimacy thrives in an atmosphere of emotional intimacy where everything is open and the focus is on giving, not receiving. Several years ago I (Larry) counseled a couple who were struggling with sexual conflict. The root of the problem surfaced in the first ten minutes of counseling. Though Rhonda and Herb had been married over twelve years, they both had little or no understanding of their different sexual responses. And Herb made it clear that he really didn't care. He just wanted to fix the problem.

Good communication is crucial to good sex. Tell your mate what you like and dislike. Couples who depend on subtle signals to communicate their sexual interest may run into conflict. Signals are often misinterpreted or unclear. Couples who create a loving atmosphere find a welcome place to share their desires without fear of rejection.

As you set your goals, here are some helps to remember:

- Sex is a God-given gift in marriage to be prized and enjoyed.
- If you have children or hectic lifestyles, planning times of lovemaking together may be necessary, but use creativity and spontaneity. Don't be too predictable. Prepare your place, wherever it is, with thoughtfulness and love. Do you prefer a cozy evening by the fire? Friday night love-in? Kitchen interlude? Mid-day excursion? Early morning wake-up call?
- Make your lovemaking an all-day event, with numerous sprinklings of affirmation, word gifts, and thoughtful actions building anticipation throughout the day.
- Talk about your love together. Then celebrate it joyfully.

The Exercise

Is your lovemaking all you want it to be? How can you enjoy it more as God's gift to you? Answer these exercises honestly and share your answers together.

1. Three ways you give me pleasure in lovemaking.

2. Three ways you can make our lovemaking more enjoyable for me.

The Plan

Three things I'm willing to do to make our lovemaking mutually satisfying.

1.

2.

3.

Spiritual Intimacy Exercises

Back to Basic Values

Let's find the hidden values
That somehow slipped away
And work on what's important.
Let's do it now—today!

The Exercise Goal

To establish mutual values in our marriage.

The Biblical Idea

Ever since God created Adam and Eve, values have been an important part of married life. The Tree of the Knowledge of Good and Evil in the Garden of Eden symbolized a standard of values for this first couple. When they disobeyed God and chose Satan's values instead, the light in their marriage—fellowship with God—went out. Their decision set off a chain reaction. Confusion and turmoil followed as marriages and families began to function abnormally.

Later in the Old Testament, God established a system of morals, beginning with the Ten Commandments. Laws against adultery, murder, lying, stealing, and idolatry represent only a few of God's values. The Book of Proverbs provides a set of principles that brings success to those who follow them. Honesty, trust, hard work, tolerance, love, thriftiness, moral purity, and loyalty are some of the values recommended by King Solomon. But it was Jesus who breathed life into old values and gave us a reason—eternal life—to live by his principles. His love freed us to have fellowship with God again, something that laws couldn't begin to accomplish. Jesus came, holding up and fulfilling his heavenly Father's standards. Only through a personal relationship with him can couples please God. Only through Christ can couples begin to find God's good and perfect values for their marriages. Those values could be summarized in this verse: "Be not conformed to this world: but be . . . transformed by the renewing of your mind" (Rom. 12:2 KJV).

The Need

Christian couples need to have Christian values in order to live a fulfilled life and please God.

Stephen Grunlun, author of *Marriage and the Family*, says perhaps the two best indicators of a couple's values are how they spend their money and how they spend their time. Someone has said, "Show me a man's checkbook and datebook and I will tell you what kind of man he is."

Caught up in a subtle spiral of materialism, success, and "me-first" philosophy, couples may find Christian values slipping away. A mobile society has scooped out wide gaps between the generations, and the effects of parents' and grandparents' traditional support and wisdom are fast disappearing. Couples can make a commitment, however, to join the growing number of families that are opting for a back-to-the-basics approach to life. After we commit to Christian values, we can then plan ways to maintain them.

The Exercise

Do the following exercises alone, then share them with your mate. You may discover that while you are a penny-pincher who prefers a used, economy car, your spouse loves new Cadillacs. Notice any wide discrepancies in your values. These may be areas of conflict you should discuss and work on in the future.

1. List what you think are the ten most important values in life.

2. On a scale of one to ten, rate each value according to its importance.

The Plan

List the three most important values that you both agree on. How can you help each other follow them?

1.

2.

3.

List three values you disagree on. Plan to follow one person's values or plan on a compromise you can both live with in good conscience. Discuss how your values can become more biblical.

1.

2.

3.

∽ *10* ∽
Spiritual Leadership

You don't have to preach like Peter
Or even pray like Paul;
Just lift our family to the Lord
And seek him first, that's all.

The Exercise Goal

To establish and maintain spiritual leadership in our home.

The Biblical Idea

In the Old Testament, God gave the Jewish father the responsibility of leading his family in spiritual instruction and worship. Why was it necessary to teach God's principles to children? It ensured a generation who would love the Lord with all their hearts, souls, and minds. It preserved the faith.

Parents are still in the discipleship business with their children. We are not to delegate that responsibility to others.

Although Scripture doesn't specifically command the husband, "Thou shalt be the spiritual leader of the home," it does say, "Fathers . . . bring them [children] up in the training and instruction of the Lord" (Eph. 6:4). The principle of leadership is firmly established. Ephesians 5 indicates that a husband is to love his wife as Christ loved the church. That signifies a nurturing, protective spiritual relationship. As protector and priest of his home, a husband can help lead his wife and children into a strong, growing relationship with Jesus. But both husband and wife are partners in this important task. Working together, they can make a powerful team.

The Need

Women crave spiritual leadership from their husbands. Children, too, long for the security and love found in a home where God is not a profane name, but a household word of love and respect.

Some men have never assumed the role of spiritual leader. In these cases, subtle hints from the wife—such as leaving a marked Bible open on his nightstand, taping Scripture verses on the bathroom mirror, or sneaking a copy of Dobson's book, *What Wives Wish Their Husbands Knew About Women,* into his suitcase the next time he travels—usually don't help. Finding the root of the leadership problem can lead to solving the problem.

Sometimes a husband may feel inadequate and abandon his role, especially if he thinks his wife is more spiritually mature than he is. He may fear rejection if he doesn't measure up to her standards. Here is where communication of feelings, fears, and desires is so important.

Shared responsibilities in spiritual teaching, prayer, or devotions can lend creativity and closeness to the marriage. Even the children can play a part in spiritual training. From the mouths of babes God has initiated both humorous and thought-provoking lessons for the family. But a pushy or know-it-all attitude in either mate will turn off the other one, as well as the children.

Because one of my (Becky's) spiritual gifts is teaching, I usually have approached spiritual leadership in concrete ways such as teaching our girls Scripture memorization with alphabet index cards, using exaggeration, association, and repetition. Larry's balance as an encourager has helped me see that parental modeling and life experiences often provide the best spiritual leadership.

Our girls often associate God's faithfulness and provision with practical times—such as when our cars conked out and God sent angels in disguise either at just the right moment or with just the right car part—much more than with any lessons we formally taught them. Parents who can turn everyday events into miracles for their children will usually find captive audiences. Those lessons are not quickly forgotten.

The Exercise

Do the following exercises individually and share the answers together.

1. Who is currently the spiritual leader of your family?

2. Describe the spiritual leadership in your family of origin.

3. Three things I think spiritual leadership should include.

4. Three things I like that you are doing to help lead us spiritually in our home.

The Plan

Based on your discussion of your answers, determine how your family will be led spiritually. Then write down three ways you are willing to help your family grow spiritually.

1.

2.

3.

⚘ *11* ⚘
Faith and Beliefs

I see a mountain looming,
Coming closer every day.
A seed of faith is all we've got;
We'd better plant today!

The Exercise Goal

To stretch our faith and together trust God for his provisions.

The Biblical Idea

Faith is like a muscle. If we use it, the muscle strengthens. If we don't, it sags and weakens. How much faith do we need? A houseful? A cupful? A thimbleful? Jesus says faith the size of a mustard seed will move the most impossible mountain (Matt. 17:20).

No faith? No problem! "Faith cometh by hearing, and hearing by the word of God" (Rom. 10:17 KJV). Whatever the need, God has a provision. Check out his promises. Are you afraid to give your money or time or family to God? He challenges you to test and prove his faithfulness (Mal. 3:10). Are you facing difficulties? Challenges? Need wisdom? Ask! (James 1:5).

Faith needs an object. God has a proven track record for faithfulness. The couple who share a mutual faith in Jesus Christ and who look to him for every provision will find themselves developing mighty muscles that can withstand great pressure.

The Need

Most of us remember times of faith testing. Looking back on those experiences strengthens our belief in God's faithfulness. Recently I (Becky) spent several hours reviewing my journals from the past few years. Details of unexpected expenses, empty bank accounts,

42

parental crises, ministry problems, and personal battles filled the pages. For most of them, I could stamp "ANSWERED" across the page. Seeing God's provision in those situations encouraged me to stamp "STILL TRUSTING" across any problems yet unresolved.

For several years, we've also kept a "blessing catcher," a notebook where we record spiritual or material blessings God sends our way. From sales of our writing to restored health, we can find reminders that our Redeemer is faithful and true.

Couples who are willing to make their marriages a lifelong walk of faith will find a rare adventure, second to none.

The Exercise

1. How long has it been since you and your mate asked God for something specific?

2. Three ways God has been faithful to us in the past.

3. What are you trusting in God for right now?

4. Three areas in which I have difficulty exercising faith.

5. Three obstacles to my faith.

The Plan

After discussing your answers, plan how to trust God together for all your needs.

1. Three new areas in which I want us to trust in God.

2. Things to do that will strengthen our faith.

∾ 12 ∾
Prayer

We've tried to handle problems
Just doing as we please.
Perhaps it's time to stop and spend
Some time down on our knees.

The Exercise Goal

To make prayer a priority in our marriage.

The Biblical Idea

Jesus knew the power of prayer. He rose early, stayed up late, and escaped often to spend time with his heavenly Father. Jesus needed the intimate fellowship of prayer to strengthen him for his earthly mission.

James 5:16 could apply well to marriage: "The prayer of a righteous man [couple] is powerful and effective." With so many marriages and families under attack, prayer is a vital force, our all-out offensive weapon against the "foxes that spoil" a union. In Ephesians 6, Paul says to pray on all occasions with all kinds of prayers—praise prayers, Help! prayers, confession prayers, protection prayers, thanksgiving prayers, petition prayers. Marriages are at risk without the protective power of prayer.

Marriage should be two lives intertwined with strands of love, held together with sturdy seams of prayer. Robert Hall says, "Prayer serves as an edge and border to preserve the web of life from unraveling."[1] If marriages must hang on by a thread, let it be the thread of prayer.

The Need

As we look back over the years, we believe that prayer has been a key to keeping our marriage alive and growing. In the earlier years of our marriage, we prayed together primarily at mealtimes, crises, and during family devotions. But several years ago, we began praying together—just the two of us—before bedtime. That intimate fellowship with God helped us through disappointments, personal failures, and our daughters' adolescent years. We learned the power of praise as well. Prayer took us to the throne room of God, into his presence.

At times, we heeded Jesus' reprimand to his disciples: This kind requires fasting and prayer (see Mark 9:29 KJV) and we intensified our prayer efforts accordingly. Prayer has not eliminated problems for our family, but it has fortified us internally and increased our dependence on the Lord.

Prayer is not an option. It is not only a command, but also our right and privilege as God's children. Ron Dunn says, "We are not beggars cowering at the back door, pleading for a handout. We are children seated at the Father's table."[2]

The Exercise

First complete your own answers to the exercises; then share your lists.

1. Three things I would like you to pray for me about.

2. Three things I would like us to pray for ourselves about.

3. Three areas in which I would like to see our prayer life improve.

The Plan

Discuss how you will make prayer a priority in your home.

1. Times we will pray together.

2. Obstacles in our prayer life.

3. Ways we can overcome the obstacles.

∽ *13* ∽
Bible Study

It's time to change our diet—
Milk alone won't do.
Let's eat some meat and vegetables—
A hearty spiritual stew!

The Exercise Goal

To increase spiritual unity and growth through individual and joint Bible study.

The Biblical Idea

Just as a baby needs milk to grow, so does the Christian. "Like new-born babies," says 1 Peter 2:2, "crave pure spiritual milk, so that by it you may grow up in your salvation." However, no child could thrive on milk alone. Gradually, parents add fruit, cereals, vegetables, and meats to the baby's diet. Lest we become like the carnal Christians in 1 Corinthians 3:2, still infants in Christ, not able to digest solid food, we must add spiritual meat to our diets in order to spur spiritual growth.

One couple in the Bible, Aquila and Priscilla, were known for their spiritual maturity. Both were teachers, both tentmakers, both committed to spiritual growth. Like the psalmist, they used God's Word as a lamp to their feet and a light for their paths (Ps. 119:105).

The Need

Some couples can hardly find time for studying the Bible alone, much less together. Pressures of work, school, children, and even church responsibilities choke out quiet moments. Yet most recognize the need for a strong value system and spiritual growth that comes only from a plan of Bible study, meditation, and even memorization. So what's the answer?

Tailor your own schedule. We all make time for what is important in our lives. Begin by expressing your desire to the Lord. Then take some action. It may mean getting up earlier, staying up later, or carving out some time from your lunch hour. You won't find much unused time lying around, so make your own.

Holding each other accountable is effective for some couples. Becky and I separately used one particular workbook style Bible study, then shared answers and thoughts from it once a week. During a particularly tough time in our ministry and in parenting, we took one noon hour a week for a Bible study on wisdom. The insights we discovered encouraged us to keep our eyes focused on God, not on our circumstances.

Let your own needs dictate your choice of Bible study. Read the Bible through while taking notes. Study characters or character qualities. Whatever you choose, just do it! You won't be satisfied with a liquid diet anymore.

The Exercise

What are your personal Bible study habits? How can you foster spiritual oneness through Bible study? Think about the following questions and share your answers together.

1. One thing that keeps me from being consistent in Bible study.

2. Three ways you could encourage me in my own personal Bible study.

3. Three subjects I would like for us to study in the Bible together.

The Plan

Discuss when, where, and how you will study the Bible, together and alone.

	Together	Alone
Frequency		
Time		
Topic/Book		
Where		

∽ 14 ∽
Family Devotions

Where have all the heroes gone?
The joys of innocence that once were known?
Lord, make us strong as families.
Turn our hearts toward home.

The Exercise Goal

To plan for devotional experiences that promote spiritual unity in the family.

The Biblical Idea

Deuteronomy 6:6–8 is a well of wisdom we can all drink from as we travel the sometimes dry and dusty road that leads to spiritual vitality in the family:

> These commandments that I give you today are to be upon your hearts. Impress them on your children. Talk about them when you sit at home and when you walk along the road, when you lie down and when you get up. Tie them as symbols on your hands and bind them on your foreheads. Write them on the doorframes of your houses and on your gates.

That covers all the bases, doesn't it? When you're at home, when you're away, when you go to bed, and when you get up. Experiencing God in family life is a lifestyle. It's the natural sharing of spiritual truth that encourages and builds up family members. It's warm and comfortable, not rigid and judgmental.

So who initiates this? Who fosters this warm atmosphere and stimulates conversations about God? Deuteronomy 6 points to parents who have these words on their hearts. Chuck Swindoll says, "Truth is more permanently transferred from a parent's life than his lips. Modeling the truth far outweighs preaching it to the young."[3]

Jesus used both natural and structured opportunities to teach his "family" of disciples. At times, he gathered them around himself like a mother hen with her chicks. He frequently used parables—stories with familiar objects or scenes—to teach lasting truths. He built godly character in these men so they could, in turn, disciple the world for Christ.

The Need

Foreign gods surrounded the Israelite families in the time of Deuteronomy. Doubtless, these Hebrew kids were enticed to reject their faith. Our children face the same temptations. The gods are different, but the allure is the same. Instead of worshiping wooden or stone idols, our kids are tempted by materialism, drugs, or sex. Surrounding our children with positive examples and godly heroes can be challenging but is not impossible. It's important to start while they're young.

Authors and therapists Drs. Brian and Deborah Newman use a variety of creative ways to lead their two young children in family devotions. One of their favorites is acting out a Bible story using simple props. Brian loves to dramatize the story of the lame man, especially when he's tired. Debi's pregnancy was a perfect time for her to play the part of Sarah, Mary, or Elizabeth.

Denalyn Lucado, wife of best-selling author and pastor Max Lucado, believes that modeling our faith is the best teaching tool. But she also uses fun evening devotions to teach her girls lessons about God. Dale Hanson Bourke relates one example of Denalyn's creative devotions:

> When she was teaching the girls about God providing manna for the children of Israel, she hid vanilla wafers on top of the ceiling fan blades in their bedroom. When the time came in the story to illustrate God's goodness, Max hit the switch and cookies flew across the room. Denalyn is the kind of mom who would worry about the crumbs later.[4]

Making time for structured family devotions is difficult because many busy families rarely gather for mealtimes together at home. But whether it's mealtime moments, bedtime gatherings, or daily spiritual conversations, families need the cohesiveness that shared devotions bring.

The Exercise

Think about your own family now and your family of origin. What part have family devotions played in your life? After some reflection, answer the following questions; then share your answers.

1. Describe your family devotions, if you had them, in your family of origin. Were devotions structured, natural, or life-experience teachings?

2. One suggestion I have for our family devotions.

3. Some ways I am willing to share in this responsibility.

The Plan

After discussing your answers, plan your family's devotional life.

1. Compile your ideas for family devotions and decide who will be responsible for what. In what order will you follow ideas?

2. Decide when you will have structured devotional time with your family.

3. Discuss how your conversations can be more spiritually oriented.

Just-for-Fun Exercises

∽ 15 ∽
Fun and Laughter

To love and cherish until death
Was really only half
Of what our wedding vows entailed:
We should have pledged to laugh.

The Exercise Goal

To add fun and laughter to our marriage.

The Biblical Idea

Proverbs 17:22 says, "A cheerful heart is good medicine." And nowhere is that fun-loving spirit needed more than in marriage.

God must have thoroughly enjoyed creating the world. Can you imagine what fun he had forming the world out of nothing? To speak the sun and moon into existence and spray-paint the heavens with millions of shining stars? To hollow out the mountains and valleys with one swoop? To form a man and woman from the dust of the earth?

Jesus, too, enjoyed life. He made room in his life for fun—wedding celebrations, playing with children, friendly conversations, and maybe even fishing!

The Need

We hear couples complaining often about the lack of time for fun. Operating on overload, couples feel the pinch of relentless schedules. Worries choke out good old-fashioned fun. And too often, couples stop smiling a week after the honeymoon. The pizazz that made the relationship so much fun begins to fizzle.

When we first tried this exercise on developing fun and laughter, we realized how serious we'd become. Whether it's as ridiculous as tickling matches, as practical as regular golfing dates, or as simple as pointing out a great line from the comic strips, couples need fun.

Steve and Beverly often add humor into their marriage to diffuse anger. Private signals, jokes, or messages break up tense moments with laughter. Sharon says of her comical husband David, "Just add David and water—instant humor!"

Ray Hildebrand once penned the song, "Get to Doing What You're Happy Doing." Life is too short and far too complicated. We like one couple's motto: "A giggle a day keeps the therapist away."[5] Laughter really is good medicine. A spoonful of fun and laughter makes love go 'round!

The Exercise

On separate sheets of paper, do the following exercises alone. Then exchange lists.

1. Three things we're doing that add fun to our marriage.

2. Three fun things we used to do together.

The Plan

List three things you would like to do in the future to add fun and laughter to your marriage. Include ideas that would make humor part of your daily life. Set dates for activities. Have fun!

1.

2.

3.

∞ *16* ∞
Rest and Recreation

All work and no play
Puts us to the test.
We need some time to ease our minds,
A chance to stop and rest.

The Exercise Goal

To plan relaxing times of recreation in our marriage.

The Biblical Idea

Few couples in the '90s would agree with Solomon's words in Ecclesiastes 3:1: "There is a time for everything, and a season for every activity under heaven." A time to be born? Yes. A time to die? Yes. A time to work? Yes. But a time for rest and relaxation? No way! We've got too much to do!

God designed one day of the week as a rest day, a break in the work week to honor him and to rest our bodies. Many times during the week, Jesus knew he had to get away from the crowds to draw strength and refreshment from his heavenly Father. Those breaks nourished his spirit as well as his body.

The Need

Employers have found that short breaks increase their employees' production and creativity. Our bodies, minds, and spirits need times of refreshment. Working seventy to eighty hours a week without rest and recreation is an invitation to emotional and physical meltdown. God did not create us for endless production.

Dr. Richard A. Swenson, author of *Margin*, says this about work, time pressures, and the need for recreation:

Work has invaded evenings, nights, weekends, holidays, and worship days. Stores and restaurants that once respected margin respect it no longer, often open twenty-four hours a day, 365 days a year.

Harvard economist Juliet Schor explains that the average American will work the equivalent of one month longer this year than twenty years ago.[6]

Marriage partners who neither play together nor even take recreational time for themselves are like volcanoes ready to erupt. Recreation literally re-creates in us an appreciation for God's creation. It renews and revitalizes our ability to see and think clearly.

Whether pursuing a sport or working together on enjoyable projects, couples who establish common recreational goals together early in their marriage will find a natural, increased intimacy in the empty nest years.

The Exercise

Think about your likes and dislikes in recreation. What is recreation to you? What kinds of things do you like to do together? Apart? Then answer the following questions separately before sharing your answers.

1. Three things we once did together for recreation that I enjoyed.

2. Three things I would like to do personally for recreation.

3. Three recreational activities I would like for us to do together in the future.

The Plan

Take this opportunity to schedule some recreation times. They can be regular or one-time events.

1. Recreation _____

   Date and time _____

2. Recreation _____

   Date and time _____

3. Recreation _____

   Date and time _____

∽ 17 ∽
Favorite Foods

A French cafe with Cordon Bleu,
Frozen TV dinners just for two . . .
How about a change tonight?
I'll cook a special meal for you.

The Exercise Goal

To add variety and spice to our relationship by creating fun food experiences.

The Biblical Idea

Making food a fun experience is for Americans a phenomenon unique to the last generation or two. I (Larry) remember my dad's commentary on the subject. "Food is food," he would laughingly say. There were no frills or thrills in his Depression-era experience. Our recent culture has transformed food into an adventure.

The idea of eating as a pleasurable experience, however, is not new to Scripture. Venison and goat may not head your list of gourmet delights, but Isaac loved them. According to Genesis 27:14, "He [Esau] went and got them [in this case, goats] and brought them to his mother [Rebekah], and she prepared some tasty food, just the way his father liked it." Enjoying some of his favorite foods was such a pleasant experience, it was among Isaac's last requests before his death.

The Need

Food can be a common denominator for a variety of experiences you can have as a couple. Have you ever tried chili and cheesecake? That was the weird combination resulting from our first progressive dinner date. We started out at a great Southwestern restaurant of my

(Larry's) choosing for our appetizer of chili and cheese and wound up at Becky's request, a quaint French cafe, with strawberry cheesecake for dessert. You can choose different restaurants for each course, with the number of courses depending on how much money is in your recreation budget—and how long your antacid lasts.

Don't limit your food fun to restaurants, however. Planning a gourmet cooking night at home or surprising your mate by preparing or bringing in his or her favorite meal is a great way to spice up your times together.

Don't let limited budgets or diets spoil your fun. Some of our favorite food experiences have been sampling the freebie foods at a local health food market, as well as at a nearby, large discount food chain.

For the health conscious, check out a sugar-free or low-fat cookbook from your library and plan two or three weeks of fun menus. One couple we know admits that preparing healthy food is challenging. To add variety to their meal planning, they often toss a week's worth of nutritious menus into a hat and then take turns drawing one out each day.

Also, sharing responsibilities makes the work easier and the experience more enjoyable. Whatever you do, be creative, have fun, and eat heartily!

The Exercise

Try out the exercises below by working on your own lists individually, and then share your responses with your spouse. Think outside the lines. Use your creativity. There are some culinary delights out there just waiting to be sampled!

1. Three of my favorite foods.

2. A dining experience we've tried that I would like to repeat.

3. My idea of the ultimate dining experience.

The Plan

Plan fun food experiences for your marriage. Write down three dining treats you would like to try, who will be responsible for them, and when they'll happen.

1. _____

   Who's responsible_____

   When we'll do it _____

2. _____

   Who's responsible_____

   When we'll do it _____

3. _____

   Who's responsible_____

   When we'll do it _____

❦ 18 ❦
Vacations and Retreats

I hear the beaches calling
And maybe mountains, too.
Any place we get away
Is paradise with you.

The Exercise Goal

To plan special getaways that strengthen us physically and emotionally as a couple and as a family.

The Biblical Idea

A look at the shepherd in Psalm 23 finds him leading us sheep beside still waters where he restores our souls. Still waters indicate a quiet, peaceful place—a place of retreat and drawing away for a time.

The Hebrew root word for *restore* means "to turn back, or to relieve or refresh." God knows we need a time to pull away. How important it is to stop the clock for a while and bask in the joys of marriage together. Anticipating their honeymoon, Solomon's bride said, "Take me away with you. . . . Come away, my lover" (Song of Songs 1:4; 8:14). If we need to spend time away together on a honeymoon, how much more should we retreat often and relive those joys repeatedly?

The Need

Scores of couples have never taken a vacation or gone on a retreat together alone. "Too expensive!" "We have kids!" "Too many work pressures!" "No time!" There are all sorts of excuses given for staying home. We heard Paul Burleson, a pastor and evangelist in Oklahoma, offer a prescription for couples: "Divert daily, withdraw

60

weekly, and abandon annually." A retreat can be a weekend or a weeknight. And vacations don't always require money.

When the girls were still toddlers, we started taking our own private marriage retreats to the beach, back to our honeymoon spot, or just overnight in a beautiful hotel several miles from home. Your getaway may or may not be a quiet place, but it should be one that brings restoration and refreshment. If you're like us and sometimes have to rest from your vacations, you may need to reevaluate your next vacation agenda to make sure it's restful.

Be sure to budget for those trips and plan both couple and family vacations at least once a year. Our family has camped together in national parks, buried each other on sandy beaches, hiked up mountain trails, and fished together in beautiful lakes. We've scoured flea markets, shopped the malls, and tubed in the snow. Decide what you can afford and plan accordingly.

Do you have a tight budget? We'll never forget how God provided a San Diego vacation one year when we couldn't afford it. One morning a money order appeared in our mailbox—mail manna from heaven from an anonymous giver—for just the amount we needed for our vacation. Where there's love, there's a way, even if you don't receive anonymous donations.

Why do we need to escape? Distractions like phone, friends, television, and home responsibilities dull the cutting edge of our relationship. Just a few days away can sharpen our focus and trim away unnecessary worries. And if you think you can't afford it, think again. If you value your marriage and family, you can't afford not to.

The Exercise

Think about the kind of vacations you'd like to take as a couple and as a family, if you have children. Complete the exercises below and share your lists together.

1. Three places I'd like to go on a vacation or retreat together as a couple.

2. Three places I'd like to go as a family.

3. Three places I'd rather not go.

The Plan

Discuss your lists. If your idea of vacation differs from your mate's, work toward a compromise. Don't forget to set some definite get-away goals. Remember how important physical and emotional refreshment is.

1. Where we'll go _____

   When _____

   Just us or family _____

2. Where we'll go _____

   When _____

   Just us or family _____

3. Where we'll go _____

   When _____

   Just us or family _____

⧢ 19 ⧢
Luxuries

I've thought of the Bahamas,
A romantic cruise for two,
But if money's short, then time from you
And a bubble bath will do!

The Exercise Goal

To add extravagance or luxury to our marriage.

The Biblical Idea

When David inquired about buying a threshing floor from Arau-nah the Jebusite so he could build an altar to the Lord, Araunah said, "No. You can't pay me for anything. I'll *give* you not only the thresh-ing floor, but the materials for the altar and even the oxen for the offering" (our paraphrase).

King David refused. "I will not sacrifice to the LORD my God burnt offerings that cost me nothing" (2 Sam. 24:24).

Extravagance, or second-mile love that costs us something, is not an unfamiliar theme in Scripture. From King David's purchase of the threshing floor, to the building of Solomon's temple, to the expen-sive gift of God's own Son, we see the price tag God placed on love. We may not consider the widow's mite to be a luxurious gift, but it cost her everything she had.

Paul reminds us of God's extravagance to his children: "Now to him who is able to do immeasurably more than all we ask or imag-ine . . ." (Eph. 3:20). Love lavishes itself on the object of its affection. Marriage is a good place to follow God's example.

63

The Need

Second-mile love, the extravagant side of marriage, is a rare and beautiful thing. Second-mile love is not last year's recycled valentine. It's not offering our mate secondhand promises or leftover time. Extravagance may not be expensive, but it should cost us above and beyond what is expected.

Extravagance may mean a once-in-a-lifetime vacation to Hawaii, the planning of which could be complete with evenings to study brochures, chart out travels, and shop together for new clothes. Extravagance may also mean washing the dishes and drawing a hot bubble bath for your wife or treating each other with a long-over-due block of time together.

One husband we know hired a maid for his wife. Another whisked his mate away for a weekend at a quaint bed-and-breakfast inn. One couple who is in the process of rebuilding their marriage considers marriage counseling to be one of their finest luxuries.

As small children, our girls often returned from Christmas shopping with no money left. We were tempted to lecture them for spending too much, until we realized what they had done. They had emptied their pockets for the ones they loved.

Extravagance empties its emotional, physical, and spiritual pockets to lavish love on another in a way that brings pleasure both to the giver and the receiver.

The Exercise

1. An extravagant way you shared your love with me in the past.

2. Three luxuries we can't afford, but ones that I would love to have or save for.

3. One luxury I would like that costs more in time than money.

The Plan

After discussing your answers, make a secret list of three ways you will add extravagance to your marriage by lavishly giving to your mate.

1.

2.

3.

One luxury we'll start saving for together _____

∞ 20 ∞
Adventures

If Grandma Moses painted,
Then honey, so can I!
But she was in her eighties,
Can I wait a while to try?

The Exercise Goal

To stretch our horizons by adding adventure to our lives.

The Biblical Idea

If we could talk with the Bible heroes of our faith, we'd probably find a common chord running through their lives: Knowing God is an adventure! Can you top these?

- "Power"-walking on dry land through the Red Sea (Exod. 14)
- A three-day cruise in the belly of a whale (Jonah 1–2)
- A midnight walk on the water (Matt. 14)
- A prison breakout (Acts 16)
- A first-round knockout of the world's heavyweight champion (1 Sam. 17)
- A marathon wrestling match with an angel (Gen. 32)
- A slumber party in a lion's den (Dan. 6)

God delights in the impossible and spares nothing to accomplish it. He turned pansies into prophets and paupers into princes. The apostle Paul summed up his own life this way: "To me to live is Christ" (Phil. 1:21). To Paul, Christianity spelled a lifelong adventure.

The Need

All of us need times when we break out of the mold. We need to expand our worlds and stretch our minds in order to grow as individuals and couples. Challenges strengthen us. Getting out of our expected patterns of life and off our eight-to-five, merry-go-round existence may mean moving to a remote country spot. It may mean a college course to challenge your brain, a river-rafting expedition to get your adrenaline pumping, a new hairstyle, a two-week overseas mission trip, or service in a homeless shelter on Thanksgiving.

I (Becky) never will forget the exhilaration of skiing with Larry for the first time. My one descent without falling was great! Some adventures are once-only experiences, like the time Cindy tried raw oysters to fulfill a dare, or when Lyndon and Candy flew under a bridge in a two-seater plane! Others are keepers, like raising kids!

Someone has said the best way to conquer your fears is to deliberately face them. Whether your adventure is a purposeful effort to reduce your fear or an unconscious attempt to complete a childhood dream, go for it! The only limits are your budget, your health, and maybe your time. A one-hundred-year-old man recently accomplished his first bungee jump. What's your excuse?

Remember your purpose is not to grab all the gusto you can. Like our Bible heroes, your call from the Lord may entail an adventure. Use any adventure to draw you together in some challenging experiences. Let marriage and life itself be the adventure.

The Exercise

1. One adventure I remember from the past.

2. One adventure I'd like to try personally.

3. One adventure I'd like for us to attempt together.

The Plan

Discuss how adventure can stimulate your marriage. Think what your response would be if the Lord called you to a really big adventure. Plan three dates for challenging experiences.

1. Challenge _____

   Date to attempt_____

2. Challenge _____

   Date to attempt_____

3. Challenge _____

   Date to attempt_____

∽ 21 ∾
Hobbies

Stamp collecting's not my thing,
And you find reading boring.
There must be something we can do
That doesn't leave us snoring!

The Exercise Goal

To encourage balance in our lives, individually and together, through hobbies.

The Biblical Idea

Proverbs 31 pictures a well-rounded woman, one who makes time for herself, her husband, children, and others. She's industrious, wise, and mentally alert. Her husband apparently is balanced and happy as well and has a good reputation at the city gates, or marketplace, of the town.

Proverbs 15:13 says that a happy heart makes a cheerful face. Those who maintain balance in their lives show it in their countenance. The workaholic, driven to perform, may see no need for worthless pursuits such as hobbies. But having fun is important, too. Hobbies are like coffee breaks in our lives that bring smiles to our hearts and give us a cheerful outlook.

The Need

Hobbies may simply be recreation, adding fun to your life, but some consider them to be diversions that inspire, enlighten, or enlarge their world and their relationships.

Sharon and David are fortunate to share the same hobby. Since both are talented in art, they broadened their interests after marriage and started watercolor painting together. One of their favorite memories is when David kidnapped Sharon and took her to a luxurious hotel with a private, scenic view. He packed away the watercolor paints and easel as an additional surprise so they could capture the view permanently. That weekend, they created more than beautiful pictures; they painted indelible memories and smiles on each other's hearts.

Are you a collector? Do you collect coins, dolls, stamps, antiques? Share it together, and it's twice as nice. Are you the intellectual type? Reading together, taking new classes together, or sharing ideas stimulates some couples. Do you find joy in the outdoors, in sports, birdwatching, gardening? Anything you share together gives you a greater chance for intimacy.

What if your tastes are different? Find hobbies that interest you individually and pursue them as long as they don't create an "exit" from closeness and lock out your partner. Friends of the same sex who share similar hobbies sharpen us "as iron sharpens iron" (Prov. 27:17). But don't negate the possibility of compromise. Find something you like to do together and show some interest in your partner's activities. Brag about your spouse for that hole in one! Rave about that new recipe your gourmet cook prepared!

I don't share Larry's enthusiasm for outdoors shows, outdoors magazines, and fishing lures, but I do love to fish. He doesn't enjoy fiction as I do, but he listens to my synopsis of the latest sequel and enjoys biographies. We are discovering ways of making our hobbies an unexpected bonus and a source of mutual enjoyment.

The Exercise

1. A hobby I enjoy doing myself (or with a friend).

2. A hobby I would enjoy trying together.

3. Three ways I'll try to show more interest in your hobby.

The Plan

To add balance in your lives, plan to try some hobbies. Write down one hobby you'll do together, one with a friend (optional), and one individually. Be sure to include a starting date. Appreciate each other's interests.

1. Hobby to do together_____

   When we'll start _____

2. Hobby to do with a friend _____

   When we'll start _____

3. Hobby to do by myself_____

   When I'll start _____

Communication Exercises

∞ 22 ∞
Communication Skills

I'd like to share my feelings,
But fear makes me balk.
I wonder, could we set aside
Some time to really talk?

The Exercise Goal

To strengthen our communication skills as a couple.

The Biblical Idea

Who would have thought that such a small, inconspicuous part of our bodies could pack such a wallop? Scripture uses two conflicting metaphors regarding the tongue: The Book of Proverbs compares it to a tree of life; but James calls it a consuming fire. Try chewing on these other biblical tidbits: A fool, Proverbs says, blurts out everything he knows and answers without listening. Colossians 4:6 says to speak words that are seasoned with grace. Ephesians 4:29 suggests we offer encouraging words, and Ephesians 4:15 exhorts us to speak the truth in love.

Study Jesus' style of communication. He listened without interrupting, defending himself, or attacking others. He gave affirmation often, spoke without condemning, challenged listeners with questions, waited for ideal timing, and forgave without hesitation.

The Need

When we began working at our marriage intentionally, the problem of communication emerged as one of our toughest mountains to climb. We set a weekly time for talking. What did we talk about? Everything: feelings, likes and dislikes, calendar plans, and issues such as you'll find in this book. We avoided the negative subjects that brought instant conflict (and tears), at least for a while. We concentrated on creating a loving and encouraging atmosphere for growth. In the process we had to learn some basic communication skills such as listening without interrupting, eliminating distractions, and learning to express positive *and* negative feelings without fear of being misunderstood.

Most couples Larry counsels find communication just as challenging as we did. Two exercises that have helped us are what some call "fast-food communication" and "shielded anger." The first one you'll overhear at any fast-food restaurant. You go to the drive-thru and call out your food choices: "We'd like two hamburgers, two large fries, and two diet cokes, please."

Over the speaker comes the echo: "Okay. You want two hamburgers, two large fries, and two diet cokes. Is that right?"

"Yes" (or "No," if they misunderstood).

"Will there be anything else?"

"No" (or "Yes," if you think of something else).

When couples use this method, sometimes called mirroring or rephrasing, they are working to understand what is really being said. Practicing this method often helps us serve as a counselor to our own spouse, drawing out hidden feelings.

"Shielded anger" is a good communication exercise that helps diffuse conflict. By inviting the Holy Spirit to be a protective shield around you, you can remain untouched by your mate's words, however angry or hurtful they seem. Each partner takes turns sharing his or her feelings and cannot interrupt until the other finishes. Couples using this exercise will find this effective if they refuse to defend themselves or take the feelings personally. And always in expressing feelings, remember to say what you are feeling, with "I" statements, not with attacking "you" statements. "When we don't spend much time together, sometimes I feel lonely" sounds less threatening than "You never spend any time with me!" or "When you help me with the bills (housework, etc.), I feel less pressure" is less threatening than "You never help me do anything around here!"

We were not born with the skills of communication. We had to learn how to talk. We all have the ability to learn, but good communication takes time and work.

The Exercise

Do the following exercises alone, then compare your answers and set meaningful goals that will help strengthen your communication together as a couple.

1. Three things I learned about communication from my family of origin.

2. Three ways I feel we communicate well as a couple.

3. Three weaknesses in our communication skills.

The Plan

Discuss your answers. Determine the communication problems in your backgrounds and in your marriage that you need to overcome. Review the ideas in this chapter and list three ways you can improve communication in your marriage.

1.

2.

3.

∞ 23 ∞
Affirmations and Encouragement

Thoughtful words, a little praise,
Positive affirmations,
Build a home with sturdy bricks
Upon a strong foundation.

The Exercise Goal

To build a sturdy foundation of love by encouraging and affirming my mate.

The Biblical Idea

To encourage has long been considered one of the most charitable things one Christian can do for another. That was the motive behind Paul's exhortation to the Thessalonian believers: "Therefore encourage one another and build each other up, just as in fact you are doing" (1 Thess. 5:11). Paul knew the pressures these Christians faced. He had heard about the threat of persecution. To counter the barrage of difficulties, Paul implored them to encourage and build up one another.

Another word in the New Testament used in similar contexts is *edify*. It comes from two Greek words: one that means "a home" and the other, "to build." To edify literally means "to build a home." As you edify your mate, you are constructing your marriage, building a rock-solid foundation for your home out of love and consideration.

The Need

The writer of Proverbs said wisely, "A word aptly spoken is like apples of gold in settings of silver" (Prov. 25:11). Affirming words are also strong bricks that build esteem in our mates, especially when we offer them with precise timing—like when Becky has just put on her dress and is looking at herself in the mirror with that "I-sure-don't-look-as-good-in-this-as-I-used-to" look on her face. Bingo! What an opportune moment to reassure her that I still find her extremely attractive. Or when I'm staring at my to-do list with that "I'll-never-get-all-of-this-done" look on my face, it's a great time for Becky to give me a word of thanks and encouragement for working to provide for her and the family.

I remember a time in our marriage when I had resigned my position on our church staff and was trying to determine what God really wanted me to be doing. I felt discouraged and was wrestling with self-doubt. Becky and I were sitting on the couch in the den one night shortly after my resignation, when she turned to me and said, "You know, you're really awesome."

"I am?"

She began to enumerate the ways she considered me to be a blessing in life: the ways I supported her, the strength she drew from me, my sensitivity to the children, my wisdom as a spiritual leader. She piled up "apples of gold in settings of silver" on me that refreshed and brightened me in a way that nothing else could have done. I got up the next morning ready to face the future with confidence.

In his book *The Language of Love* Gary Smalley shares a powerful way to encourage others through word pictures. Embellishing similes such as, "You're like a diamond jewel that sparkles and shines" or a modern parable that amplifies what a treasure your mate is are among hundreds of ways to strengthen the foundation of love. Word pictures that paint "I love you," warm hugs that say "I care," or special winks that say "You're special" are all blocks of love to build up your mate.

The Exercise

Answer the following questions together.

1. Three things that encourage me.

2. Three ways you have affirmed me in the past.

3. A word picture that describes how I feel about you.

The Plan

Discuss your answers. Make a building plan for your foundation of love by writing down three ways you can encourage and praise your mate. Include when you will say and do these things.

1.

2.

3.

∽ **24** ∽
Feelings

*It's hard to understand you
If I don't know how you feel.
Can we take off all the masks
And find out what is real?*

The Exercise Goal

To understand each other better by sharing our feelings with each other.

The Biblical Idea

Throughout Scripture we see a range of emotions: the confusion of Job, the exhilaration of Solomon and his bride, the jealousy of Joseph's brothers, the joy of those touched by Jesus, the fear of Jesus' disciples, the gratefulness of Paul for his friends. Even Jesus himself felt the joy of fellowship, the sadness of departure, and the pain of suffering.

Some couples are skilled at hiding their emotions. When David tried to hide his feelings of guilt, it affected his health (Ps. 32:3). Proverbs 14:13 says, "Even in laughter the heart may ache." God knew the physical, emotional, and spiritual value of confession and expression.

Proverbs 20:5 says that the purposes of a person's (our mate's) heart are like deep waters, and only a person of understanding can draw them out. God wants us to go fishing, to probe beneath the surface and help draw out those feelings in each other. Only then can we truly understand one another.

The Need

How do you begin to break down barriers to communication? Before trying to understand what your mate feels, work at identifying your own feelings. How can you draw out those buried emotions? How do you share your own feelings without fear of rejection?

Try doing a ten-minute check-in often: Find a place to relax, then examine your feelings and share them with each other. Take turns paraphrasing the feelings your mate expresses to you and encourage your spouse to keep going until you get to the root problem. This process takes frequency and patience; don't expect to arrive at the core of your feelings the first time.

When I (Becky) write greeting cards, I try to put myself in the receivers' shoes in order to understand what they are feeling during certain circumstances and to empathize with their sorrow, loneliness, or joy. Doing this in your marriage will help create emotional intimacy.

The Exercise

Think about what you are feeling at this moment. Do the following exercises and share together.

1. Identify all the positive emotions you are feeling at present or have felt in the last week.

2. List any negative emotions you may be feeling or have felt in the last week.

3. Take off any masks you're wearing and share an emotion or feeling that you may or may not have shared with your mate before. Use these suggestions if you need to.
   a. A time when I felt afraid.
   b. A time when I felt disappointed.
   c. A time when I felt excited.

The Plan

Set up dates and times for check-in times you can use to share your feelings with each other, thereby understanding each other better.

1. Date _____

    Time _____

2. Date _____

    Time _____

3. Date _____

    Time _____

∽ 25 ∽
Expectations and Hopes

You were my knight in shining armor,
I was your queen for a day,
But when the castle crumbled,
Our dreams all washed away.

The Exercise Goal

To identify our marriage expectations, communicate them to each other kindly, and evaluate them.

The Biblical Idea

After several years of marriage, some of us may feel like Job, who cried out to God in the midst of physical and emotional suffering: "He tears me down on every side till I am gone; he uproots my hope like a tree" (Job 19:10). Job's expectations of prosperity and health had been shattered, uprooted, and turned upside down by a tidal wave of destruction. Life had not turned out the way he had expected.

If Zipporah (Moses' wife), Simon Peter's wife, or any of the other disciples' wives had known where their husbands' faith would lead them, would they have had second thoughts about marrying these guys? If they had dreamed of permanent roots in a nice condo by the sea, a private cruise on the Mediterranean, or undivided loyalties from their men, they probably were disappointed. God uprooted their lives as well.

King David failed to communicate expectations and desires to his family. He waited until a family tragedy took place— the death of his son Absalom—to identify and express his emotions (see 2 Samuel 13–18). Wise couples learn to share expectations in a positive way before problems or crises push emotions to the breaking point.

The Need

Before marriage, most couples form their own conceptions of the ideal partner. Based on Hollywood images or qualities they remember from parents, they mentally project an image of what their mate will be like. I (Larry) have counseled many people who expected their spouse to mirror their parents' model behavior or to complete their unfinished business with a parent who failed to nurture them adequately.

A couple who looks to each other to supply their every need will end up smothering the flames of marriage. No human being can meet all of our expectations. Helping to fill those needs we can meet requires concentration and, like everything else in marriage, deliberate work.

I remember one night a few years ago when Becky clearly communicated how I had not met her expectations. She had planned to fly out for a writer's conference in Phoenix the next day and was preparing a manuscript to take with her. She had waited until the night before to print her manuscript at the community college nearby. The entire night was a disaster! Everything that could go wrong did. She returned home that night with an unfinished manuscript, on the verge of tears.

When she related her story to me, my response was totally different than what she expected. What she wanted was understanding, a little sympathy, and a shoulder to cry on. What she got was a lecture on her poor planning, with a reminder about her habit of not leaving herself adequate time for such things.

The cascade of tears and angry words that followed told me that I had not fulfilled Becky's hopes. Talking about it, identifying the expectations, and acknowledging my lack of understanding helped reconcile us.

Some experts suggest we give up our expectations, particularly in marriage. That may be true sometimes, but to surrender expectations without acknowledging them could mean to deny their existence. Perhaps *exchanging* them for other expectations is a better idea. Learn to accept each other's flaws. Change what you can about yourself, and exchange what you can't change about your mate, letting God meet your expectations in himself.

When a mate does disappoint us—and it will happen, no matter how considerate we are—how blessed is the couple who can forgive and cry out with the psalmist, "My hope, my expectation, is in you, Lord" (Ps. 39:7, our paraphrase). Expectations are real, but realizing them rests in our relationship with Christ, who is our hope of glory. Only he can meet our deepest needs and expectations.

The Exercise

What did you expect when you married your spouse? June Cleaver? Cindy Crawford? Gourmet dining every night? Tom Cruise? A debt-free home? Flawless kids? Complete these exercises and share your answers.

1. Three marriage expectations that have been met.

2. Three marriage expectations that have not been met.

The Plan

1. Identify the expectations you individually have of your marriage. List them here and share them together. Discuss if they should be realized or exchanged.

2. List three things you are willing to work on to help meet the expectations you are able to meet.

❧ 26 ❧
Habits and Pet Peeves

You squeeze the toothpaste in the middle,
But I start at the end.
You're neat, I'm not; You're cold, I'm hot!
Where do we begin?

The Exercise Goal

To better understand our differences and work together at eliminating bad habits.

The Biblical Idea

As someone aptly said, "If two people in a marriage are exactly alike, one of them is unnecessary." Like delicate snowflakes, God created each one of us unique in personality, temperament, and abilities. Proverbs 24:3 says, "By wisdom a house is built, and through understanding it is established." When we each take the time to understand the reasons for our mate's behavior, we add more bricks to our foundation of love.

It's one thing to understand the motives behind our actions, another to change a bad habit. James 1:23–24 talks about one who looks at his face in a mirror, then leaves, forgetting his character and appearance. That's the picture of a spouse who refuses to change. Colossians 3 tells us to throw away the old habits and harmful attitudes—the crutches that keep us from walking victoriously in the Spirit in gentleness, love, and understanding.

When love overlooks a multitude of faults (1 Peter 4:8), it is not blind to the faults, pretending they don't exist. Neither does love simply wish them away. Love probes to understand the reason for the faults and then looks beyond the faults to the possibility of change. (However, the person who marries with the hope of changing a

84

spouse may be severely disappointed.) While we can't change another person—only God can do that—we can work together to mutually confess our faults and change our hurtful behaviors.

The Need

Couples often find after marriage that opposites attack, not attract. The bad habits they form or carry over from childhood tend to push out the things they have in common. Quirks overlooked in the dating stages soon turn to pet peeves. Marriages can come unglued over petty habits such as dropping dirty socks in the middle of the living-room floor and cleaning closets only when the door won't close anymore.

"That's the way I am" won't cut it in marriage. "I can't change" means "I won't change." Larry has an incredibly organized mind that functions by lists and order. Although I like neatness and cleanliness, I operate more on the "My mess, my office, my business!" motto. How do we deal with our opposite behaviors? (Often!) One way is by better understanding ourselves. He's a perfectionist; creativity is more important to me. During one particularly intense session, we talked through these differences, repeatedly mirroring each other's statements until we got down to the root of the problem.

"In ministry," Larry said, "I operate with the awareness that there is always a need not met, a hurt not healed, a person not touched. To come home and see 'nests' or clutter reminds me there's even more to do as soon as I get home."

Even though I felt differently, I realized I could honor what was important to him. So, we compromise. I try to keep my "nests" more organized or out of sight, and he cleans out the pantry or the closet since I feel that is a waste of creative time. My office is still my territory to clutter as I wish.

Sometimes it's our attitude or response toward our mate that changes. To those couples who let pet peeves drive them crazy, we offer you the advice given to us by some counselor friends, Lois and Dixon: "If it bugs you, it's your problem!"

And to all you middle-of-the-tube squeezers, sock-droppers, and nit-pickers: You can change with God's love and your patience with each other. Bad habits are like grains of sand that grind away at the marriage foundation. Habits formed in a lifetime don't change overnight. The choice is yours. Do you want a house built on love or sand?

The Exercise

Think about your own pet peeves and both your own and your mate's bad habits or even differences. Ask God to give you a heart open to change. Then do the following exercises alone and spend some time sharing together.

1. Three ways you're different from me that I appreciate.

2. Three pet peeves I have about you.

3. Three bad habits of my own that I'm willing to work on.

The Plan

Compile and discuss your lists. Try to understand the reasons for the differences you have. Write down ways you can modify your differences out of kindness to each other. Then write down how you will overcome your own bad habits.

1. Differences _____

   How change_____

2. Bad habits _____

   How change_____

∽ 27 ∽
Anger

I sulk, you steam; I cry, you scream!
How about a compromise?
Let's go to separate corners
Until our anger dies.

The Exercise Goal

To deal with anger in a constructive way.

The Biblical Idea

Many of us grew up believing that all anger is a sin. Yet even Jesus got angry. With one swipe of his hand, he sent pigeons flying, tables crashing, and money boxes clanging to the floor. Wide-eyed merchants stared in disbelief at the actions of this otherwise gentle carpenter.

Jesus released anger many ways—through a stinging rebuke, direct confrontation, or gentle reprimand—yet without sin. With the money changers in the temple, Jesus responded in the only language they could understand. When it came to defending his father's reputation, Jesus stepped forward.

Most of our anger does not originate in righteous indignation, however, or in defending our Father's reputation like Jesus did. Ideally, Paul's words in Colossians 3:8 challenge us to "Rid yourselves of . . . anger." When anger does surface in your relationships, how can you deal with it constructively?

Scripture gives at least two guidelines that might help. Timing is important. Ephesians 4:26–27 says, "'In your anger, do not sin': Do not let the sun go down while you are still angry, and do not give the devil a foothold." In other words, don't harbor anger and let it seethe like hot lava until it erupts in an explosion, splattering whoever is

nearby. Anger left untended sours quickly into bitterness and resentment, opening the door to Satan's activity in your life and marriage.

Select words carefully. Proverbs 15:1 encourages us to respond
gently. Cruel, harsh words only provoke more anger. They are like
poison darts. When they hit their intended target, few anti-toxins
can heal the damage.

The Need

Anger is usually a secondary emotion, therefore we encourage
couples to unearth the root beneath the anger. Are you feeling threat-
ened? Attacked? Fearful? Disappointed? Rejected? Why?

In the past, Larry and I took pride in never having had an argu-
ment. To me, submission meant silent surrender. This only sent
anger underground, however. Whenever I felt strong emotions well
up in me, I would either sulk in silence and deny any anger or I would
whimper like a wounded puppy.

Years later when those suppressed feelings surfaced, we began
working on new responses, on my being heard and understood. We
learned to acknowledge both positive and negative feelings in ourselves, but for me that meant unlearning my tendency to deny or
cry.

We're still learning how to vent anger constructively. I have difficulty labeling and admitting my angry emotions, but now we take
more time to help each other dig down to the root problem.

The Exercise

Think about and answer the following questions alone. Then
share your answers with each other.

1. Three ways we usually dealt with anger in my family of origin.

2. In what situations do I sometimes feel anger?

3. How do we usually handle anger?

4. A time recently when I felt anger toward you, and how I responded.

The Plan

To help you deal with anger constructively, discuss the above answers, then complete the following statement.

When one of us is feeling angry, I would like for us to _____

_____

_____

_____

∾ 28 ∾
Conflict

You're hot under the collar—
The steam is coming through.
I think you'd better cool a while
Before I talk to you.

The Exercise Goal

To identify sources of conflict and work toward resolving them.

The Biblical Idea

A twin who stole his brother's birthright (Gen. 25), a wife who outwitted her drunken husband (1 Sam. 25), and a father who tried to kill his own son (1 Sam. 20)—remind you of modern TV dramas? Where can you find more conflict than in the Bible? Some people handled it wisely. Others, like the Pharisees who were rebuked by Jesus for their hypocrisy, stormed away in anger and plotted their revenge.

When some Jews were teaching to the new Gentile converts that circumcision was necessary to salvation, a conflict erupted between them on one side and Paul and Barnabas on the other (Acts 15). They couldn't arrive at a solution, so they called in a mediator. Paul and Barnabas appointed a council to go to Jerusalem to discuss the problem, avoiding what could have been a major catastrophe. The council met with the leaders of the church and allowed each side time to state its arguments. Finally, when James presented a compromise to the entire assembly, the people listened and accepted it.

Does that sound too easy? Other Bible figures didn't handle conflict quite so well. When Zipporah and Moses failed to agree, she ran home to Mama. Even Paul and Barnabas argued: Paul, defiant about taking John Mark with him on a journey because of John Mark's earlier failure, left Barnabas with the responsibility of caring for John Mark.

Conflict resolution may not be possible all the time. But Romans 12:18 says that when it is, "As far as it depends on you, live at peace with everyone."

The Need

Failing to acknowledge our disagreements or refusing to deal with conflicts only aggravates the problems later. Sometimes couples need to plan a later time to deal with a heated subject more objectively.

Conflict is inevitable but not always harmful. Gerald Foley says, "Couples too often play it safe, avoiding conflict and the wounds that may occur. They don't confront the issues, and their relationship doesn't grow. If, after years of marriage, we have no scars from dealing with conflict, we need to ask ourselves, 'Was there nothing worth fighting for?'"[7]

Couples emerge from separate backgrounds with different ideas, values, and attitudes and are bound to butt heads eventually. Remember that you're created unique! On some issues you may both be so adamant, you will have to agree to disagree.

When handling conflict, deal with issues honestly. If you reach a stalemate, be open to a mediator—get counseling. I (Larry) tell young married couples one of the best gifts they can give their mates is to promise to go to counseling at any point that either partner feels it necessary. And always, present your solutions or problems to God in prayer.

The Exercise

Complete the exercises below. Prayerfully commit a time to work on conflict resolution. Use your projected goals to reflect mutual steps of action for resolving the conflict.

1. Three ways I usually deal with conflict.

2. List any recent disagreement or conflict.

3. Choose one conflict which you'd like to work on together. Then list three possible solutions to it.

The Plan

Discuss your answers. Use the following guide to help you resolve the conflict or conflicts you have identified. Use this plan each time you meet to discuss conflicts.

1. What I will do _____

   What you will do _____

   When we will prayerfully discuss this again _____

2. What I will do _____

   What you will do _____

   When we will prayerfully discuss this again _____

3. What I will do _____

   What you will do _____

   When we will prayerfully discuss this again _____

∞ 29 ∞
Strengths and Weaknesses

You overlook my failures;
You're strong when I am weak.
Together, we can form a team.
God made us both unique!

The Exercise Goal

To appreciate each other more by identifying our strengths and weaknesses.

The Biblical Idea

Psalm 139 reminds us of our uniqueness as individuals. God fashioned no carbon-copy couples; neither are there perfect mates. Throughout Scripture God used imperfect people, men and women such as Martha, Moses, Peter, and the disciples. Each had strengths, but they were obviously weak in other areas.

In 1 Peter 3, Peter lists the beautiful strengths of a godly woman, including a gentle and quiet spirit—not Peter's strength for sure! If he was describing his wife here, we can see how her strengths made up for his obvious weaknesses. Probably only someone like Peter's wife could have lived with this bold, bumbling apostle.

Romans 12 shares a list of spiritual gifts—supernatural abilities that God gives to each of his children. Whereas some Bible couples appear to have shared the same gifts (Aquila and Priscilla both were teachers and encouragers), other couples differed. But they were powerful coworkers for God as they pooled their resources in ministry.

The Need

Whether you married a singing sanguine, a moody melancholy, a practical phlegmatic, or a clashing choleric, as we've said before, chances are your mate is not like you. The way you handle problems, the way you approach challenges, even the way you face temptation may differ at times.

It's important for couples to understand not only their differences as men and women, but also their strengths and weaknesses as individuals. Are you a perfectionist or a messie? A left brain or a right brain? A thinker or a doer?

At a marriage enrichment leadership training weekend, with only one evening to prepare an entire marriage retreat, Larry and I eagerly dove into the project. As a creative melancholy, I wanted to add flair, alliteration, and originality to the retreat topics. I needed a large chunk of time. Larry, a sensible phlegmatic, preferred to stick with familiar, practical subjects since time was limited.

Four hours into our planning, at 1:30 A.M., we finally cried "uncle" and broke down in laughter, realizing we were placing undue stress on ourselves and our relationship. After being married almost thirty years, we're still discovering how different we are. Each day brings new challenges that require us to pool our strengths and weaknesses into workable solutions.

Invariably through the years, when one of us is weak, the other has been a tower of strength. We approach problems from our individual point of view according to the gifts and temperaments God has given us.

Accentuate the positive, but allow for the negative. Couples can avoid much unnecessary conflict by giving each other permission to fail. A nod of acknowledgment to our mate's humanness can motivate him or her in ways criticism might never achieve. Of course, you can keep pecking away at each other. But who likes to feel like a plucked chicken?

The Exercise

Make a comprehensive list of your own strengths and weaknesses, perhaps including your temperament and your spiritual gifts (if you know what they are). Then answer the following questions and exchange lists. Be open and non-defensive when you hear your own weaknesses.

1. Three of my greatest weaknesses.

2. Three of my greatest strengths.

3. List what you think are your mate's three greatest weaknesses.

4. List what you think are your mate's greatest strengths.

The Plan

After discussing your lists, plan to be more understanding of your mate in light of his or her strengths and weaknesses.

1. Discuss how your strengths and weaknesses complement each other.

2. Do a study together on spiritual gifts.

3. Discuss how you can acknowledge each other's humanness rather than criticize each other's faults.

Heavy-Duty Exercises

∞ 30 ∞
Family Background

You may think you know me well,
But there's more than what you see.
For when you married me, my dear,
You wed my family tree.

The Exercise Goal

To understand ourselves and our mates better by looking at our family backgrounds.

The Biblical Idea

One day some dissenting Pharisees began to challenge Jesus' testimony and authority (John 8). "Who's going to believe you? You don't have any witnesses. Your testimony is invalid!" Jewish law required two witnesses to prove the validity of a claim. Jesus wisely responded: "My testimony stands for two reasons: I know where I came from and I know where I'm going" (our paraphrases).

Jesus knew his roots. Because he knew his Father well, he had no identity crisis, no questions about his behavior. Jesus' family background affected his every action and thought.

Throughout Scripture we see the influence of family backgrounds. Jacob inherited his mother's tendency toward deceit, while Timothy reaped the blessings of a godly mother's and grandmother's modeling. Whether through temperament, habits, physical features, beliefs, or parental teaching, children are influenced by their family of origin.

The Need

Someone has wisely said that when we marry, we marry not one person, but the person's whole family too. Each of us is a composite picture of parents, grandparents, and siblings. We each bring bags of garbage as well as hidden treasures into our marriage. Why do you want five kids and your spouse only two? Why do you get angry when your mate is ill? Why is one of you a cheapskate and the other a giver? What makes you and your mate tick? Do you both, like Jesus, know where you came from and where you are going?

If you want to really understand your partner, take time to probe into the past. Spend an afternoon or evening asking your spouse questions about his or her background. What things were taught? What attitudes were caught? What were the strengths and weaknesses of the parents? If there is dysfunction in your life or marriage, examine your background. Dysfunction often begets dysfunction until someone breaks the chain.

We've shared openly with each other and with our children as much about ourselves as we can. When we've traced a pattern in our children (such as perfectionism) back to ourselves, we tell them this: "Now that you know where it comes from, it's your responsibility to correct it. We'll help all we can. But you can no longer say, 'It's my parent's fault!'"

Communication brings understanding. And when we understand, we can begin to solve problems.

The Exercise

Journey back through your childhood and mentally observe your family background. Write down your thoughts, answer these questions, and share them together.

1. Three of the greatest influences of my childhood.

2. Three factors in my family background that affected me positively.

3. Three factors in my family background that affected me negatively.

The Plan

For several weeks, keep a journal of memories as you recall your childhood. Set a time in the future to come back together and share any insights on how your family of origin has affected you in other ways. If it would help, make a list of questions to ask your mate about his or her family background.

∾ 31 ∾
Roles and Responsibilities

Your turn to take the garbage out!
Your turn to do the dishes!
Let's take the time to talk about
Our roles and all our wishes.

The Exercise Goal

To define roles and create a balance of responsibilities that make our marriage a true partnership.

The Biblical Idea

As you define marriage roles and responsibilities, Philippians 2:2 offers a good rule of thumb: "Make my joy complete by being like-minded, having the same love, being one in spirit and purpose." Although Scripture categorizes some responsibilities such as protection and provision as more peculiar to men, and others such as nurturing and mothering to women, it also emphasizes oneness in the marriage relationship. While giving separate guidelines for husbands and wives in Ephesians 5, the Bible encourages us to work together as teammates. God gives us freedom to work out our roles as long as they bring harmony to the home and honor to him. What works for one couple may not work for another.

The Need

With the increase of two-income families today, couples face growing struggles defining roles and responsibilities. For those operating in traditional roles, some household tasks appear to be clear-cut: meal-planning, shopping, and cleaning for women; home and car repairs and financial planning for men. We know one wife, however, who happens to be an excellent plumber. She is mechanically gifted and loves a challenge. Another husband and wife work together as firefighters. We have some friends who stretched traditional roles even farther: When the children were small, Lloyd sewed (and designed) much of the family's wardrobe. Sylvia loved it!

Although we consider ourselves fairly traditional in our roles, Becky and I have learned to share more responsibilities, particularly since she began writing full time. I tackle car and home maintenance. Becky sets up the budget and keeps the books, but we do the financial planning and bill paying together. Sometimes I help her clean; sometimes she helps me in the yard.

Debi Newman describes her husband's training in unconventional roles: "From an early age Brian did a lot of the cooking and grocery shopping. Even cleaning. He's very good at what you normally associate as a housewife's chores. In my house, Mom did most of that and she didn't need any help." Brian's doing an ordinary task such as grocery shopping was threatening to Debi. She continues, "It took me a long time to realize, and then to accept, that the roles tradition assigns to marriage are nothing more than guidelines. My mom did all the shopping in our home. Brian's family of origin was much different, giving him a much different body of experience from mine."[8]

Some couples like written agreements that delegate household tasks and parenting responsibilities. We prefer verbal compromise or sharing as the need arises, but we do plan some jobs. Whatever works for you is the direction to go. God gives each of us different gifts, and doing the tasks that fit your abilities brings the most satisfaction.

Here are a few words of caution:

1. Disputes over some responsibilities often reveal hidden differences. Be wary of power or control issues.
2. Be honest with each other in your likes and dislikes and reasonable in your requests. Demands bring resentment; requests bring response.
3. Be open and willing to compromise. Work together to share your responsibilities in a way that meets your mutual needs as marriage partners and yet honors God's defined roles for man and wife.

The Exercise

1. Describe the roles and list the responsibilities your parents had and have.

2. List your current responsibilities.

3. List your mate's responsibilities.

The Plan

Compare your lists and negotiate a workable plan for sharing responsibilities in your marriage. Try some of our ideas if you want. Be sure to observe the list of cautions.

∽ *32* ∽
Parenting

Children are a gift from God—
My heart knows that it's true;
But whines and wails have tipped the scales—
Tonight, it's me and you.

The Exercise Goal

To achieve a satisfying balance between our parental responsibilities and our marriage relationship.

The Biblical Idea

Most of us would agree with the psalmist's view of kids as stated in Psalm 127:3–4 (NASB): "Behold, children are a gift of the LORD: The fruit of the womb is a reward." Scripture echoes that sentiment many times. From Genesis, where God's first words on the subject are to be fruitful and multiply and fill the earth, the Bible has been bullish on children. The psalmist adds, "How blessed is the man whose quiver is full of them" (Ps. 127:5 NASB).

Some Bible parents might have agreed, however, that at times children are a pain, not a pleasure. Eli's two sons, Hophni and Phinehas, abused their preacher's kid privileges and disregarded their father's correction. Absalom rebelled against his father, King David, and tried to steal the throne. After all Jehu had done to destroy Baal worship, his son Jehoahaz immediately reinstated it. Even Mary and Joseph felt pain when they misunderstood their son Jesus and panicked when they couldn't find him on the way home from Jerusalem.

Some parents kept an emotional balance in spite of unruly children. In Luke 15, when the prodigal son left home in rebellion, his parents allowed him to reap the consequences of his choice. There is no indication that they interrupted their lives for him or gave up on him in frustration. They never gave up hoping in, praying for, or loving their son, but the household didn't fall apart because of this parenting problem.

The Need

Probably few of us would argue with the Scripture's upbeat outlook on children and parenting. However, a wild night with the kids at your favorite restaurant can quickly cloud your perspective. The theory that "two's company, three's a crowd" can become reality, especially when the cares of raising children begin to squeeze out couple time.

Some couples make the mistake of devoting all their free time to their children. An exclusive diet of soccer games, T-ball, picnics, and trips to the zoo is a treat for the kids but may not leave much time to nurture your marriage.

I (Larry) remember the shock that registered on a young mother's face when, in a marriage counseling session, I suggested she and her husband get away together for a weekend.

"What about the kids?"

"Leave them with your parents or friends," I offered. Her look said to do so would be selfish and a disservice to her children. This mindset is usually a forerunner of problems that surface later, an indicator of an anemic and neglected marriage.

Giving our children the care they need and keeping our marriage fresh is a delicate balance to achieve. But perhaps these two priorities are not as far apart as we might think. Someone has said, "The best gift you can give your children is a mom and dad who deeply love each other." Surveys indicate that one of the leading sources of insecurity in kids today is the fear that their mom and dad will divorce. Investing time in your marriage may actually be one of the best ways to love and nurture your children.

The Exercise

Focus for a few minutes on the importance of these two priorities in your life. Then complete the exercise and share your responses with your mate.

1. Three things we've done right in parenting.

2. Three things we could do better.

3. Ways our parental obligations interfere with our marriage.

4. Ways our children enhance our marriage.

The Plan

List three things you're willing to do to bring balance between your parental and marriage relationships. Set dates, if applicable.

1.

2.

3.

∽ 33 ∽
Disciplining Children

Disciplining our children
Often grieves us to the core;
But leaving them to raise themselves
Hurts them even more.

The Exercise Goal

To agree on a plan of discipline for our children that will help them grow into responsible adults.

The Biblical Idea

Start a child in the right direction, with attention to his uniqueness, says Proverbs 22:6, and even when he is old, he will stick to that way. Children left to themselves bring dishonor to their parents, their peers, and themselves. God gives parents the duty to raise up, to nurture, and to discipline their children (Eph. 6:4), not with an iron fist or blind love, but with the instruction of the Lord.

From Spock to Dobson, parents can find a wealth of dos and don'ts on how to raise kids. Sorting out wise advice from the bookshelves can be challenging: When in doubt, check it out—in God's Word.

The Book of Proverbs itself is an adequate training manual for parents. Sex, godly friendships, good stewardship, and respect of authority are only some of the subjects Proverbs addresses, providing instructions we can use for training our children. Just as God disciplines us—his children—because he loves us, so are parents to discipline their children in love (Heb. 12:6). And what is the result of disciplined kids? Joy and respect for us as parents (Prov. 15:20; Heb. 12:9), and a harvest of peace and right living for your children.

Ultimately, our kids must make their own choices and accept the consequences of their own actions. We are responsible, however, to start them in the right direction and form them according to God's blueprint.

The Need

How you raise your children may be influenced by the way your parents raised you. In one college class I (Becky) took recently, I met several adults who had grown up in rigid, legalistic homes. Now as grown parents, they had decided to give their children room to make more of their own choices. On the other hand, another mom, who had reaped the consequences of having no dating restrictions as a teenager, vowed not to let her child date until she was eighteen.

Children tend to live up to their parents' expectations. Bruce Wilkinson, president of Walk Thru the Bible Ministries, recalls an experience involving his own son that illustrates this point. He was teaching a twelve-week series at a large church. The last night, he was asked to say something about his family. When he introduced his son, he went blank. So in a panic he said, "This is David, and he is funny; he makes everybody laugh." Not true, but it was too late. When the meeting was over, he heard a commotion and some screaming over the loudspeaker. It was David, yelling into the P-A system and making faces.

On the way home, he said to his wife, "Sweetheart, we're not going to make it as parents. Just look at what our son did."

"What did you expect him to do?" she replied.

"What do you mean, what did I expect him to do? Act a little bit more mature than that!"

His wife's words stung: "Well, didn't you tell him what you expected him to be like in front of everybody?"[9] Parental expectations are powerful.

Discipline is not a meting out of punishment, but a loving plan of action, with consequences to match the offense. Unfair or angry spankings are just as harmful as no discipline at all. Verbal abuse breeds discouragement, anger, and self-hatred. Try to agree together on how to discipline your children. Someday, they will thank you.

Somehow our children have overlooked and forgiven all of our mistakes and experiments with them—and there were many—

maybe because down deep they know we disciplined them because we really loved them.

The Exercise

How did your parents raise you? What choices were you allowed? What is your idea of effective discipline? Think about these questions and complete the following exercises. Share together a plan of action for disciplining your children.

1. My parents chose the following ways to discipline me as a child and teen.

2. As a result, I felt_____

3. Three ways I would like to improve the discipline system we use with our children.

The Plan

Compare your answers and come up with a loving plan of discipline you will both support and consistently use. Write down the steps for it here. Include offenses and consequences, number of warnings, corporal or verbal punishment, exact wording, and other details.

1.

2.

3.

∽ 34 ∽
Budgeting

We can buy it now, let's charge it!
The decision's up to you.
But what'll we use for money
Next month when bills come due?

The Exercise Goal

To create a workable budget.

The Biblical Idea

"Where does the money go?" could be the cry of the foolish man in Proverbs 21:20, the one who spends all he makes. In the parable of the wise stewards, God teaches us to be faithful with our possessions and to multiply the talents he gives us (Matt. 25:14–30). How we use our money says much about our Christianity and our commitment to God.

"Remember," Jesus says, "Your life is not the sum of your possessions" (Luke 12:15, our paraphrase). His Word warns us against the love of money and reminds us that where our treasure is, there our heart is.

Contrary to what most of us say, there is enough money to go around. There's enough, 2 Corinthians 9:8 says, to feed your family and meet your needs, with plenty left over to give your neighbor. Two of God's purposes for money are to provide for our needs and circulate his wealth. To do so, we need a plan.

The Need

At a financial planning seminar Larry and I attended a few years ago, the speaker asked how many people were using a budget. About 5 percent raised their hands.

I can remember when my dad first started giving me an allowance. I'd tuck away nickels and dimes into my labeled envelopes faithfully each week. Life was simple then! However, as a married couple, we have found the more money you make, the greater the need for a budget, a disciplined plan of spending. Each year we trace the previous year's spending patterns by recording month by month all expenditures. We find an average of what we spent that year, add a percentage for increased cost of living, and formulate a new budget.

It takes discipline to say, "That's not in the budget." But what a joy it is to approach vacation time, Christmas, or a special opportunity to give and say, "Yes! It's there." Does the budget work? Yes and no. Surgery wiped out a budgeted vacation one year, and unexpected repairs have made adjustments necessary also. But otherwise, we have learned to "just say no" rather than pull out the plastic card and purchase impulsively.

We recommend any books or resources on financial planning by Larry Burkett or Ron Blue. They both share practical planning strategies for operating on a budget and for good stewardship.

As you think about a budget, here are some basic suggestions to help you get started.

1. Purchase a budget book or log.
2. Chart your spending habits for the last three months through checkbook stubs or receipts.
3. Make a list of all fixed and flexible spending categories. Don't lump everything under miscellaneous. Break down your expenses if possible.
4. Record expected income for the year.
5. Remember, expenses must not exceed income. If they do, you have two options: Reduce expenses or increase income.
6. Budgeting takes teamwork and discipline. Your plan may look good on paper, but it requires accountability on all items and mutual decisions on most items.
7. Be willing to negotiate any item that brings disagreement. If a budget sounds too confining, try allotting a small "mad money allowance" for each of you in addition to your budgeted items.

The Exercise

Prayerfully consider your stewardship habits. Answer the following questions, then share lists.

1. Three things or attitudes I learned about money from my family of origin.

2. Three good things about our spending habits.

3. Three ways we can improve our overall spending habits.

The Plan

If you have a budget, review it together. Use the guidelines in this chapter to evaluate it. If you don't have a budget, plan one. Make a list individually of items you think belong on a budget. Exchange and compare lists and compromise on flexible items. Follow our budget suggestions or others you may prefer.

⚬ 35 ⚬
Saving Money

Penny-pinching thriftiness
May not be in vogue,
But creditors will never come
And tell us what we owe!

The Exercise Goal

To formulate a practical savings plan.

The Biblical Idea

Have you noticed how practical the Book of Proverbs is? Proverbs 13:11 says, "Dishonest money dwindles away, but he who gathers money little by little makes it grow." A wise couple plans well, like the ant, storing up food for the winter.

That doesn't mean we hoard, like the rich fool in Luke 12, depending on our own resources instead of God's. The fool's plan for saving meant moving his wealth to a bigger barn bank. But God expects us to live as wise stewards. He owns everything anyway. We're just channels of his wealth, allowing it to flow out to others to further his work.

The Need

Wise couples begin saving early in their marriage, even if it's only a small percentage of their income. Financial experts differ on how much you should save. Even a small amount establishes the habit of laying aside funds and not indulging every whim.

Starting married life with a mortgage, one or two car payments, and a house full of furniture purchased on credit seems to be the norm for many newlyweds. When sickness, repairs, pregnancy, or other unexpected expenses come, they have no recourse but liquidation or help from relatives.

We met Tony and Debbie in a church where we served formerly. They constantly struggled financially until one of their parents died, leaving a sizable inheritance. Though I'm sure they thought about saving and investing for the future, the lure of the immediate overcame them. A new Cadillac was one item on a long list of things they couldn't live without, and within months they were stuck once again in a quagmire of debt.

The discipline of saving is more important than the amount. God will give you wisdom on what to save for and how much to save. The ultimate goal of savings is not to accumulate wealth. A savings plan will help us pay cash for necessities as well as luxuries. It can also provide a cash flow for emergencies, retirement, or special gifts to others or to God's work. Material wealth is unimportant, but wise stewardship and a freedom from debt leave us time to enjoy life and become rich in the things that really count.

The Exercise

1. How did my family of origin affect my current savings habits?

2. Three reasons I think we should save.

3. Three things for which I'd like us to save.

4. Three things I'm willing to do to help maintain a savings plan.

The Plan

Project your own savings goals. Decide how much you're going to save, where it will come from, where you will put it, and what you will spend it on eventually.

1. How much?

2. Where from?

3. Where do we put it?

4. What will we use it for?

∽ 36 ∽
Pressure Points

Stress, pressure, heaviness?
It's time to get away.
You can call it what you want,
But I'm calling it a day.

The Exercise Goal

To identify pressure points and learn to deal positively with stress in our marriage.

The Biblical Idea

Did Jesus ever feel pressure, the kind that makes you want to run away? You can draw your own conclusions about that, but frequently after exhausting periods of ministering to people, Jesus withdrew to regroup physically and spiritually.

Surely with the incredible demands of meeting human needs and the weight of the world's sin on his shoulders, Jesus felt pressure—intense pressure. And yet, it didn't crush him. Instead, some of the most significant events in his ministry followed these periods of withdrawal and reflection. Jesus always rebounded from pressure-packed seasons in his life with resiliency and a well-defined sense of purpose.

Perhaps each of us at times can identify with the psalmist in Psalm 55:6–8: "Oh, that I had the wings of a dove! I would fly away and be at rest—I would flee far away and stay in the desert; I would hurry to my place of shelter, far from the tempest and storm." Some days we'd take wings or wheels to escape, or even settle for a big hole—any place to get away from pressure!

The Need

The pressures that married couples face come in all shapes and sizes. Deadlines, withering schedules, endless demands, relentless expectations—these are the all-too-familiar circumstances involving pressure. Seldom do the responses to pressure (irritability, anger, impatience, depression) show up faster than in the daily interaction of husband and wife.

Handling pressure successfully includes identifying its source. No, not by naming your boss as the bad guy, but by naming what you are feeling about what your boss said to you today and by defining what you believe about your circumstances. Ultimately what you believe about yourself, God, and your situation is the real source of pressure—and the real key to handling it well.

- What do you believe about yourself: that you can't make a mistake; that you can't function without people's approval?
- What do you believe about God: that he is in control; that he is trustworthy?
- What do you believe about your circumstances: that you'll never get through this; that nothing is going to change?

Handling pressure well means identifying your feelings; naming the belief that triggered the feelings; and finally, outlining some steps of action to relieve the pressure, stabilize your emotions, and correct your belief system.

The Exercise

1. Pressure points in my life right now and three emotions I'm experiencing.

2. Three wrong beliefs that may be contributing to my feelings of pressure.

3. Three ways I'd like to handle pressure (stress) more positively.

4. Three things you can do to help me deal with these pressures.

The Plan

Discuss your answers. Examine the pressure points you've identified. Can any be removed from your life? Can you incorporate a season of regrouping into your life? Outline a plan of action to follow during times of stress.

1. Eliminated pressures _____

2. How we will regroup _____

When? _____

3. When we are experiencing stress, we will _____

⚭ *31* ⚭
In-laws

If in-laws turn to out-laws
And invade your happiness,
When all else fails, don't give up—
Try love and tenderness.

The Exercise Goal

To develop mutually good in-law relationships.

The Biblical Idea

The Bible portrays both good and poor in-law relationships. Jacob, a deceiver himself, woke up the morning after his wedding to discover he had spent the night with the wrong bride. His own father-in-law had tricked him and given him weak-eyed Leah, Rachel's sister. Because of Laban's meddlesome and incorrigible nature, Jacob eventually left, tricking Laban out of his best livestock (Gen. 29–31). In Jacob's case, distancing himself from in-laws might have been best.

Let's look at two other in-law relationships not without their own problems, but both good examples of love and respect. Moses fostered a close kinship with his father-in-law Jethro by seeking his advice when judging the Israelite people. Jethro's counsel saved Moses from early burnout.

Perhaps the best example in Scripture of a loving in-law relationship is that between Naomi and Ruth. Having lost both husband and sons, Naomi wanted to return to her own people. Instead of staying home in the comfortable surroundings of Moab, the only place she had ever known, Ruth begged Naomi to let her live with her. Ruth's respectful love and obedience eventually led her to a new husband and a place in the lineage of Jesus. Her words to Naomi are included in today's marriage ceremonies (Ruth 1:16–17). Either Moses' or Ruth's terms with in-laws could have turned bitter or resentful without respect, effort, and love.

The Need

Many couples cringe at the mention of in-laws. Jokes abound about in-laws and "out-laws." Today's mobility has removed the benefit of the extended family's spiritual and emotional support, and couples live isolated from loved ones. Some couples who live close to in-laws struggle to find the balance between leaving and cleaving. But God intended all of our relationships to be peaceable and loving—as much as is possible.

Larry and I have both been blessed to have in-laws to whom we have grown closer through the years. We are working on this book together a week after the unexpected loss of Larry's father. I have lost not only a father-in-law, but a friend as well.

Good in-law relationships grow just as good marriages do, through intentionality. Whether brother- or sister-in-law, cousins, or parental in-laws, you can foster warm feelings through encouraging notes, visits, solicited advice, and thoughtful deeds.

The Exercise

Fill in these exercises and share your answers.

1. Three words per person that describe how I get along with each of my in-laws.

2. Three things I like about how _____ and I interact.

3. I have most difficulty with _____, because

_____.

The Plan

In order to develop mutually uplifting relationships, think of how you can serve your in-laws, as well as how you can enjoy them more. Pick out the in-laws with whom you have the most conflict and list three ways you can improve your terms with them. Add how your mate can help.

1. _____

    How mate can help _____

    _____

2. _____

    How mate can help _____

    _____

3. _____

    How mate can help _____

    _____

∽ 38 ∽
Stepfamilies and Second Marriages

Blending both our families
Is challenging for sure,
But with God's help we'll find a way
To make our love endure.

The Exercise Goal

To understand and address any problems unique to our having a stepfamily or second marriage.

The Biblical Idea

Most of the problems peculiar to stepfamilies in the Bible resulted from multiple marriages or from ungodly unions. Genesis 26:35 reveals that when Esau married Judith and Basemath, both Hittite women, they were a "source of grief to Isaac and Rebekah." Constant jealousy arose between Leah and Rachel, Jacob's wives; and between Sarah and her handmaiden, Hagar, both wives of Abraham.

And what about Joseph, Mary's husband? He had one wife but raised a son he had not fathered. Only God could give the kind of grace Joseph needed in order to understand the situation.

The Need

Couples who enter a second marriage through death or divorce and marry into a ready-made family will find a set of difficulties unlike those of other marriages. We all bring into a marriage baggage from our childhood, but these couples face the possibility of multiple problems. Yet while the potential for misunderstanding, jealousy, bitterness, and inadequacy is perhaps greater, so are the opportunities for grace, forgiveness, understanding, and love.

119

Unresolved issues from a first marriage usually reappear in the second one. Children may see a new spouse as an intruder, and a new set of parenting problems may emerge. Second marriages will face challenges, but the couple who depend on God's mercies and are willing to work through the inevitable conflicts together will find greater chances for success.

The Exercise

1. Three good things that I feel have resulted from our marriage.

2. Three trouble spots I see that have resulted from our marriage.

3. Three things I am willing to do to help us through those trouble spots.

The Plan

Set three dates to discuss any problems you might be having unique to your stepfamily or second marriage. Try to understand them as you discuss them. Decide what you can do to alleviate them.

1. Date _____

   Problems _____

   Solutions _____

2. Date _____

   Problems _____

   Solutions _____

3. Date _____

   Problems _____

   Solutions _____

Priority-Making Exercises

∞ *39* ∞

Physical Fitness

You don't have to be a "10,"
So don't get in a stew;
All I'm asking is the privilege
Of growing old with you.

The Exercise Goal

To make physical fitness and a good diet priorities as marriage partners.

The Biblical Idea

Our bodies are special pieces of equipment. This was the psalmist's perspective: "I praise you because I am fearfully and wonderfully made" (Ps. 139:14). With these intricate, complex creations of God that we call our bodies comes a responsibility, a kind of stewardship. Paul said plainly, "Do you not know that your body is a temple of the Holy Spirit, who is in you?" (1 Cor. 6:19). Paul wasn't necessarily talking about physical fitness, but he was talking about being responsible for anything and everything given to us by God.

Being physically fit is good stewardship. It's the idea Jesus taught in the parable of the talents. The faithful steward is the one who takes what he's been given and makes it even better. Keeping your body

121

physically fit is not only the right thing to do spiritually, but it's a wonderful gift to your marriage partner as well.

The Need

Former baseball great Mickey Mantle was quoted a few years ago as saying, "If I'd known I was going to live this long, I'd have taken better care of myself." We all *intend* to eat better or start that exercise program; that's why the best buys at garage sales are exercise equipment. One lady almost paid me (Larry) to take away her rowing machine. Its presence in her garage obviously reminded her of her failure to get with the program.

Fitness is one of the kindest gifts you can give your mate. No, I'm not suggesting enrolling your spouse in a health club. It's *your* fitness we're talking about. Keeping yourself physically fit says, "I love you enough to want to look good for you. I want to stay healthy and live long to make the most of our years together."

Whether you're walking, working out, or dieting, it's always easier to do it as a couple. The mutual accountability helps keep you at it. One couple we know takes physical fitness dates three noon hours a week in a local health and fitness club. I work out occasionally at lunchtime in a nearby church's Family Life Center. Sometimes Becky surprises me and meets me there. Otherwise, she tries to walk four or five times a week or do a daily fifteen-minute workout at home. At times we get so busy that we fall back into old habits; then we refocus and set new goals.

Some younger couples we know prefer active sports such as tennis, racquetball, or basketball. When our children were small, our entire family enjoyed weekly racquetball games at a nearby public park.

Because both of our fathers have had heart problems, we try to eat a low fat, low cholesterol diet. Some people excuse their eating habits by saying, "It costs too much to eat healthy." We believe it costs too much not to. And we've found that substituting fresh fruits and vegetables actually costs the same or less than junk food.

The Exercise

Jot down your responses; share and discuss them with your mate.

1. In what three areas of physical fitness do I need to be more disciplined?

2. Three ways I can encourage you to be more physically fit.

3. Three ways we need to improve our diet.

The Plan

List three things you can do as a couple to keep both of you physically fit and eating nutritiously. Include days and times for exercise.

1. Exercise _____

   Days _____

   Times _____

   Nutrition _____

2. Exercise _____

   Days _____

   Times _____

   Nutrition _____

3. Exercise _____

   Days _____

   Times _____

   Nutrition _____

Work

*To find my place in God's own scheme
And feel it matters, too,
Is second only to the joy
Of sharing it with you.*

The Exercise Goal

To better understand each other's God-given work and help make it a positive and important part of our marriage.

The Biblical Idea

Our work is important to God. In the beginning, God gave Adam a job as caretaker in the Garden of Eden. Together with his helpmate, Eve, they were to rule over God's creation. What an awesome responsibility! When God expelled them from the garden after they sinned, picking flowers turned to weed pulling, and the hard work began.

Do you remember the story of the hen who worked hard to produce food but could find no help? When all the crops were finished and the food prepared, all her friends came knocking on her door. Her response was similar to Paul's in 2 Thessalonians 3:10: "If a man will not work, he shall not eat."

God wants us to enjoy our work and to "do it heartily, as to the Lord" (Col. 3:23 KJV). God himself, when he finished his six-day work of creation, felt pride and a sense of satisfaction and said, "That's good!"

Regardless of the work you do, your marriage can make it more tolerable and meaningful, especially when the pressures pile up. As Ecclesiastes 4:9 says, "Two are better than one, because they have a good return for their work." But don't lose perspective and let work replace other priorities, as Solomon wisely reminds us: "In vain you rise early and stay up late, toiling for food to eat—for he grants sleep to those he loves" (Ps. 127:2). The key is balance.

Work is a gift. "When God gives any man wealth and possessions, and enables him to enjoy them, to accept his lot and be happy in his work—this is a gift of God" (Eccles. 5:19). Although our earthly work is temporary, to fulfill the work and purpose for which we were created—ultimately, to glorify God—is the zenith of our life, the greatest source of satisfaction. To share the joys and rewards of that labor with your mate on earth is a double blessing.

The Need

My brother shared a quotation with me that has become a favorite of mine: "To love what you do and feel that it matters—how could anything be more fun?" Can work really be fun? As a wife, what can you do to encourage your husband in his work? Does his work come between you, or is it a partnership? As a husband, do you look at your wife's work, whether she's presoaking or presiding, as an important part of your life?

Being in ministry together, though we each have a different focus, gives Larry and me a genuine sense of partnership in our work. We help each other by being a sounding board and encourager to each other.

Although I write full time at home, I've always felt my highest calling was supporting Larry and doing my part to meet the needs of my family. Larry reminded me of that one year when the kids were small. One day I complained, "I can't get my work done because of the kids!"

"They *are* your work," he said, "and mine."

My mom reassured me there would be plenty of time to write—and more to write about—when the kids were grown. She was right. When the children were young, I dabbled at writing part time, just enough to keep me happy but still maintain a household. Now that the children are grown, they're still part of our life and work, but my schedule is more flexible.

Whether you're a street sweeper or zookeeper, a lay preacher or school teacher, a homemaker or homebuilder, your work is important to God. And each of you can serve as a cheerleader for the other; just say, "I believe in you! You can do it!"

The Exercise

1. Three things I like about my work.

2. How my work negatively affects our home life and what I can do about it.

3. Three ways you can help me in my work.

4. Three ways we can improve the balance between work and the rest of our marriage.

The Plan

To better understand each other's work and make it a positive and important part of your marriage, regularly follow these three guidelines. Write under each one how you will follow it.

1. Listen

2. Cheer

3. Help

∽*41*∽
Time Management

Everybody takes a chunk
Of time from you and me.
Don't you think it's time
For us to concentrate on "we"?

The Exercise Goal

To use our time wisely so we can serve God and foster a healthy marriage relationship.

The Biblical Idea

"Teach us to number our days aright," says the psalmist in Psalm 90:12, "that we may gain a heart of wisdom." Each of us has an average of seventy-plus years on this earth. We all operate within the same system—twenty-four hours a day, seven days a week, fifty-two weeks a year.

Jesus accomplished all he needed to do in three years of ministry on earth. By concentrating on his task and building strong relationships with his disciples, Jesus succeeded in spreading Christianity throughout the world. In addition, every person he met and every need that arose became the agenda for Jesus' calendar. Dr. Richard Swenson says this about how Jesus viewed time:

Do you think Jesus would have carried a pocket calendar? Would He have consulted it before making commitments? Would He have bypassed the leper because His calendar said He was late for the Nazareth spring banquet?

Do you think Jesus would have carried a beeper? Would Martha and Mary have paged Him to come and raise Lazarus from the dead?

127

The clock and the Christ are not close friends. Imagine what God thinks of us now that we are so locked into schedules that we have locked ourselves out of the Sermon on the Mount—it is hardly possible to walk the second mile today without offending one's pocket calendar.[10]

To view time through the eyes of Christ might change our lifestyles drastically. Where do we begin?

The Need

Each one of us must manage his or her own time. "Just say no!" applies to married couples as well as to teenagers. Too many demands squeeze the life out of our relationship with each other and with God. Time is a God-given gift to use responsibly. If we relinquish the control of our time to less important commitments rather than to ones God designed, we'll find ourselves on a merry-go-round, always going in circles and arriving nowhere.

In every marriage event we lead, couples cite time management as the biggest source of frustration in their lives. We deal with this area ourselves repeatedly. We are constantly trying to examine our time commitments and reorganize them to free us up not only for availability in God's service to minister to others, but also to allow intentional time together as marriage partners and as friends.

Henry David Thoreau had the right idea. "I love a broad margin to my life," he said. "Sometimes, in a summer morning, having taken my accustomed bath, I sat in my sunny doorway from sunrise till noon, rapt in a revery." Instead of enjoying the time we do have, most of us become slaves to a clock, constantly seeking to fill the hours with activity. Perhaps one of the best things we as couples can do about time management is to abandon our clocks occasionally and enjoy an unscheduled day with those we love.

The Exercise

Spend a few moments thinking about how you use your time. If necessary, keep a weekly chart. Bring the information back and do these exercises first alone, then share the results together. After you form your plan together, take time to pray, committing it to God.

1. Three things I dislike that require my time right now.

2. Three things I would enjoy doing alone or with others if I made the time.

3. Three things I would enjoy doing together if we made the time.

4. Three ways we can make our lives more restful.

The Plan

Examine your time commitments and your answers to the exercise. List activities that you agree should not take so much time in your life and replace them with free time with your spouse, family, or God; or with activities you agree are more important.

Remove			Replace with		
His	Hers	Both	His	Hers	Both

∞ 42 ∞
Goal Setting

Our choices: moving forward,
Sitting still, or going back.
I think it's time we set some goals
To keep our love on track.

The Exercise Goal

To establish goals regularly for good, long-term couple experiences.

The Biblical Idea

Few things distracted the apostle Paul. In spite of shipwreck, imprisonment, beatings, and other traumas in his life, Paul stayed true to his goal. He spelled out that objective clearly in Philippians 3:14: "I press on toward the goal to win the prize for which God has called me heavenward in Christ Jesus." He lived for the day when he would see Jesus face-to-face, and that became the driving force and passion of his life.

Jesus never turned from his one all-consuming goal: to do the will of his Father. Disciplined and undaunted, he allowed nothing to sidetrack him. When some tried, he replied wisely, "My time has not yet come." Jesus' prayer in the Garden of Gethsemane acknowledged his successful mission: "I have brought you glory on earth by completing the work you gave me to do" (John 17:4). His words, "It is finished!" signaled the completion of the purpose for which he came.

The Need

Goals can keep us single-minded about how we relate to each other. Good intentions without actions are a poor foundation on which to build a marriage. In counseling I (Larry) have helped pick up the pieces of marriages built on words such as "sometime," "eventually," "maybe," and "probably." Good intentions are okay, but they can't fuel a lifetime together. Deciding as couples on definite goals gives our marriages forward motion. Goals help us determine where we want to go and if we're making progress. Goals make us accountable for our good intentions.

A few years ago, as part of a marriage enrichment event sponsored by our church, the leaders challenged us to develop a "growth plan" for our marriage. Becky and I picked three or four areas that we felt needed work and set some measurable goals that could stimulate growth in those areas. Then we developed immediate, secondary, and long-term steps to help get us started. A weekly check-in helped us analyze how we were doing in reaching our goals. That growth plan became such an effective tool that we now try to formulate a new one at least once or twice a year.

Goal setting can also jump-start communication about touchy issues. That may involve some work, but the results are worth the effort.

The Exercise

Although we've included opportunities to develop goals at the end of each chapter in this book, this exercise not only will help sharpen your goal-setting skills, but we hope also will illustrate its potential benefit as a regular activity. Work on this together.

1. List three long-term goals for your marriage relationship.

2. List three short-term goals for your marriage relationship.

The Plan

List immediate, secondary, and long-term steps necessary to achieve each goal you listed. Set a weekly time to review your growth plan. Then set dates to regularly review and establish goals for good couple experiences.

∞ 43 ∞
Priorities

*A dozen good things cry out
For our time and our attention.
To organize our options
We need divine intervention.*

The Exercise Goal

To establish priorities that will give stability and direction to our marriage.

The Biblical Idea

Jesus' parable of the great banquet in Luke 14 points out the narrow gaps that often exist between the ancient and the contemporary. Here are three guys in a two-thousand-year-old setting wrestling with the issue of priorities. One of life's bottom lines, both then and now, is determining what's really important. The men in Jesus' parable were each weighing a certain responsibility—surveying a piece of land, checking on some cattle, pleasing a new wife—over an invitation of greater importance.

The dilemma over priorities is a common experience in married life. It represents the nuts and bolts of determining where, when, and how we will invest our lives. Jesus knew we'd struggle and worry over that issue. That's the point of his reminder in Matthew 6:33: "But seek first his kingdom and his righteousness, and all these things will be given to you."

Making Christ our first priority is a good starting place to finding balance in our lives. Our commitment to him becomes the hub of the wheel that controls everything else. That commitment takes much of the guesswork out of setting priorities.

132

The Need

If you haven't figured it out by now, our philosophy about successful marriages is anchored in intentionality. Too many of the priorities we observe in couple's lives are the result of well-worn patterns stemming from sources other than spiritual influences. These patterns are like cattle trails that lead to empty watering holes. We follow them because they're there.

Intentionality is the pathway out. It's the road to a more satisfying approach to deciding how we as a couple will invest our lives, based not on chance or circumstance, but on what we have found is important through our relationship with Jesus Christ.

What issues need top priority? Time with God, time with your spouse, time with your children. Work, relationships, communication—any area that surfaces repeatedly as a problem, any issue that requires work and resolution, anything that's important to your life and marriage needs top priority.

The God who knows the number of hairs on our heads, the God who observes every sparrow that falls also cares about our lives and the decisions we face daily. This God will give us the time and the wisdom to establish right priorities in our lives.

The Exercise

Think through and respond to the following exercises individually. Discuss your responses together with the goal of setting intentional priorities in your marriage.

1. Look at the chapter titles in the table of contents and list ten areas or issues that you feel need high priority in your marriage.

2. Three areas or issues that you feel need the most attention.

The Plan

Discuss your responses with your mate and make these issues priorities in your marriage. List each issue and the steps you will take to make that issue important in your home.

1. Issue _____

   We will _____

2. Issue _____

   We will _____

3. Issue _____

   We will _____

Retirement Plans

Unless the kids come back to roost,
We'll have an empty nest.
Let's plan for our retirement,
And build some dreams that last.

The Exercise Goal

To plan mutual, active retirement goals.

The Biblical Idea

Retirement as we think of it is not exactly a biblical idea. Sarah and Abraham exchanged their rocking chairs for a baby crib long after most couples start drawing their pensions. Moses began his ministry at eighty. Caleb opted for mountain climbing at the same age. "But they lived longer," we argue. What about Paul? He spent his retirement in prison writing encouraging letters to the churches he had begun.

These biblical senior citizens refused to retire from serving God or to suddenly discard their chance to help others. Our idea of retirement may be to shift from giving to receiving—"I've served my time. Now I get my reward"—yet the psalmist indicates that God wants us to "flourish like a palm tree" and "bear fruit in old age" (Ps. 92:12, 14). Our bodies will wear out and retirement will include a more relaxed lifestyle because of our physical limitations, but good planning, like the preparation made by the five wise virgins in Matthew 25, will bring joyful experiences.

The Need

Most couples look forward to retirement, a time when work pressures cease and relationships grow more important. Those who have nurtured well the relationships and resources God has given will experience a season of refreshment and joy. Enjoyment of the retirement years is a natural result of careful planning throughout all the seasons of life as you look forward to discovering new things to do and enjoy.

My (Larry's) dad worked long hours on the railroad, often spending much time away from home. My mom and dad planned and saved for special times together in retirement, however. When that time came, they bought a travel trailer and vacationed at national parks and nearby mountain streams. They walked the beaches of Hawaii and marveled at the wonders of the Grand Canyon. Retirement also afforded them new ways to involve their lives in God's work and with others. Although they had only eight years of retirement together, we were amazed at the number of lives they had touched, as revealed by the response of people who ministered to my family after my father's death. My mom reaped the caring benefits of the love they both had sown in others' lives.

The Exercise

Are you a newlywed, a midlife crazy, or a late bloomer? What skills and abilities has God given you? What activities do you enjoy together? How would you like to serve God in the latter years of your life? Regardless of your age, visualize the future and answer the following questions. Then share your answers together. Don't forget to set practical steps for reaching those goals.

1. Three things I'd like to do together in retirement.

2. Three things I'd like to work on in retirement.

3. Three ways I can visualize our serving God together in retirement.

The Plan

If you are serious about your ideas, think of ways to attain your goals. Perhaps you need to talk to a financial consultant about retirement investments. List three realistic desires for the future here and what you can do now to help them be realized.

1. Dream

   Does it need a savings plan?

   Does it require new skills or education?

2. Dream

   Does it need a savings plan?

   Does it require new skills or education?

3. Dream

   Does it need a savings plan?

   Does it require new skills or education?

Emotional Health Exercises

∞45∞

Holiday Traditions

Carving, cutting, baking, singing—
Why the repetition?
I've told you once, I've told you twice:
It's a holiday tradition!

The Exercise Goal

To remember special occasions together by planning holiday traditions.

The Biblical Idea

The Old and New Testaments are both filled with traditions, each with a special significance. Building altars to celebrate spiritual markers in a person's life indicated a new experience of fellowship with God, such as Abraham's encounter with Jehovah-jireh, his provider.

The Jews celebrated a variety of holidays, including the annual Passover commemorating their exodus from years of bondage. When their children asked the reason for some of the strange traditions, their fathers replied, "So you will not forget our God's faithfulness and what he did for you." Wedding celebrations brought the tradition of delicious feasts with friends and neighbors.

Perhaps the most important of all traditions celebrated by Christians today are those observing the birth, death, and resurrection of our Lord and Savior. Christmas and Easter bring their own unique family traditions, and churches all over the world remember Jesus' sacrifice through the Lord's Supper.

The Need

Whether it's carving Grandma's Thanksgiving turkey, cutting down a live Christmas tree, writing valentines to each other, or celebrating summer family reunions together, traditions give us a feeling of security and a sense of consistency in a changing world. They are like markers, helping us remember special experiences for years to come.

Think about your own traditions—or lack of them. Traditions can include special holidays like the ones mentioned above, but don't forget others: a special date to celebrate your first kiss, a trip back to your honeymoon spot for an anniversary, a party for spiritual birthdays, maybe even celebrations of your own spiritual markers—times when you especially knew God was real. Debi and Brian celebrate their first date and the date he proposed to her. Why not create your own holiday?

Make sure your traditions don't become too complicated and squeeze out time for togetherness or the beauty of simplicity. One Christmas I (Becky) added so many traditions, I spent two weeks recuperating from exhaustion.

For several years at Thanksgiving, our family traveled on a mission trip to Mexico. There we visited with people, invited them to evangelistic movies, and talked to them about Jesus. Though we've been unable to continue that tradition, we preserve some of the memories by passing around beans at Thanksgiving. As we each take three beans, we tell three things for which we're thankful. Why beans instead of pilgrim corn? Because in Mexico, there was no usual Thanksgiving feast, only beans, tortillas, and rice.

John sends flowers to Gina and his two young daughters every Valentine's Day. At Cindy and David's house, each member gets breakfast in bed on his or her birthday. Steve and Beverly gave their only son a "Right of Passage Ceremony" celebrating his leaving of childhood into adolescence. In addition, to prepare their teenage son for dating, they arranged a "training date" with Mom. Why not try some of these ideas?

Plan traditions as a couple and as a family, but remember these three rules as you do:

1. Keep them simple.
2. Keep them fresh.
3. Keep them meaningful.

The Exercise

Make a list of traditions you remember from when you were growing up. Then complete each of these exercises alone and come back together for sharing and goal setting.

1. Three traditions I enjoyed most from my family of origin.

2. Three holiday traditions we have that are special to me.

3. Three traditions I'd like for us or our family to begin.

The Plan

List three traditions you would both like to begin. After each one, detail what is involved and who will do what.

1. Tradition _____

   Details _____

   Who will do what _____

2. Tradition _____

   Details _____

   Who will do what _____

3. Tradition _____

   Details _____

   Who will do what _____

∽ 46 ∽
Dreams

Tell me the dreams you have
Bound in your heart's cord,
And I will tell you mine. Together,
We'll give them to the Lord.

The Exercise Goal

To share with each other our heart's dreams and to work together toward fulfilling them.

The Biblical Idea

From the beginning of time, God had a dream. From that plan, or dream, God created the world: light, dark, life, color, and every living thing. Genesis 1:26 records God's dream for someone to care for his beautiful creation, for someone who would fellowship with him. God placed man and woman in a dream world, a lush paradise of flawless beauty, where they could enjoy perfect harmony with him.

Sending his Son to earth as Savior of the world—this too was God's own plan. And we, along with scores of other believers, are reaping the life-changing results of God's dream!

God wants us to dream. Psalm 37:4 says, "Delight yourself in the LORD and he will give you the desires of your heart." God delights in dreams that are inspired by him, designed to honor him and to make him look good. He wants to refine our dreams through time and experience and even counsel. God wants us ultimately to resign those dreams to him, so he can give them back, packaged with his stamp of approval.

God's dream to make Abraham father of many nations included Sarah, too. Yet when God told Abraham, Sarah laughed at the idea. Bear children at ninety? Right! Who wouldn't laugh? But from the beginning, she willingly followed her husband as they left their country, their people, and their memories behind to follow this elusive dream. When the dream was fulfilled, it was indeed a tree of life (Prov. 13:12).

The Need

My father often said, "Always have a dream" or, "Something to do today, something to look forward to tomorrow." A popular song from Rodgers and Hammerstein's musical "South Pacific" says, "You got to have a dream!" Before the reality comes the dream.

Young couples often start out with heads full of dreams and hearts full of emotions. The dreams may fade with disappointments and unexpected trials through the years. Couples must work together to keep each other's dreams alive.

Larry and I stake our lives on the promise that all things in life, good or bad, will work together for our benefit (Rom. 8:28). God convinced us of that one night on a high school date. A speeding pickup truck hit us broadside. The impact crushed the driver's side of the car just behind Larry's door. The couple in the back seat, who were huddled on the opposite side, sustained some deep cuts and bruises, but Larry and I escaped with only a minor cut or two. The highway patrolman who investigated the accident just shook his head as he looked at the twisted wreckage. "Son, I hope you realize you could have been killed." Those words were not forgotten.

The car collision that almost demolished our dreams of sharing our lives together instead prompted a new dream. Through those circumstances, Larry began to sense God calling him to full-time ministry, and this preacher's daughter became a preacher's wife. Often out of the raw emotions and experiences of our life will burst forth our message, our ministries, and our dreams. The pessimist says, "Never get your hopes up!" The optimist says, "Always have a dream!"

Twenty years ago I prayed, "Someday, Lord, I want to write a book and work together with my husband in marriage ministry." The path to fulfilling that dream has not always been easy and has at times even been painful, but God has fulfilled dreams greater than we ever could have imagined.

The Exercise

Think about your past, present, and future. Answer these questions, then share together. Let your goals be things you are each willing to do to reach those dreams together.

1. Three dreams I have for me.

2. Three dreams I have for you.

3. Three dreams I have for us together.

The Plan

Now that you've shared your dreams, work together to fulfill them. Under each of the above three categories, for each dream list three things you are willing to do, individually and together, to reach that dream.

1. Dreams for me _____

    What I can do _____

    What we can do _____

2. Dreams for you _____

    What I can do _____

    What we can do _____

3. Dreams for us _____

    What I can do _____

    What we can do _____

∞*47*∞
Friendships

We can't live in isolation;
We need a friend or two
For dinner, games, or talking—
It won't matter what we do.

The Exercise Goal

To nurture friendships both individually and as a couple.

The Biblical Idea

Friendships played an important part of Jewish life in the Bible. Men gathered in the marketplaces not only for intellectual stimulation, but also for social fellowship. Women joined together for support and for group projects such as sewing clothing for the poor. Christians gathered in homes for Bible study, for weddings, and for other social events. They thought relationships were important.

Jesus thought so too. He spent three years with an unlikely band of misfits he called his friends and disciples. They ate together, fished together, cried together, and laughed together. He valued time spent with friends such as Mary, Martha, and Lazarus in feasting, fasting, and mourning. Their lives were enriched because of the friendships Jesus formed with them on earth. Truly Jesus was a friend who loved at all times (Prov. 17:17).

The Need

Remember the children's story about the crotchety old man who thought he needed no one, whose doors remained locked to all outsiders? When his house flooded, people swarmed his doorstep with mops and brooms, lumber and paint. That crisis turned the

144

grumpy old hermit into a model neighbor. It created in him a need for others.

Our contemporary lifestyles have much of that hermit woven into their fabric. We think we can handle life alone—no need for others, no time for people's petty problems. It's easy to become self-made and self-centered. But then a crisis comes—a loved one dies, a home burns, a child is molested, a job disintegrates, a terminal illness strikes—and relationships suddenly become important.

We all need both Christian and non-Christian friends who keep us relevant, honest, and in touch with the world with which we are to share the gospel. Just as Jesus ministered by befriending others, we, too, can minister to neighbors, coworkers, or acquaintances through our friendships. Becky and I have learned about human kindness, thoughtfulness, and sincerity from our unsaved as well as our Christian friends. Whether it's a lunch partner for wives or a fishing buddy for husbands, these friends provide needed space in the marriage relationship, bring variety, and widen our interests. They enlarge our capacity to love.

Couples need couple friends as well as individual friends. Becky and I meet in a support group periodically with some couple friends who minister in other churches. Not only do we draw strength from them, but we are able to give encouragement as well. Couples who meet together for marriage support will find a place of accountability that protects them from isolation. Many times it is that feeling of isolation that prevents them from seeking out needed help before the marriage disintegrates.

In all your relationships, avoid transferring to other friendships what you should be drawing from each other. Friendships should enhance, not replace, your couple intimacy.

Friendship is a living gift from God. We can nurture it or let it die. The wise couple makes friendships a priority *before* a crisis hits.

The Exercise

Discuss your friendships. Does either of you have a problem with the other's friend or friends? Is there jealousy over time spent with friends? Does one of you need more friends? List some ways you can nurture your friendships.

1. Three ways I can nurture my relationship with my friend (individual).

2. Three ways we can nurture our relationships with (couple or couples).

3. Three things we can do together to develop new friendships.

The Plan

Discuss your answers to the exercises, then make specific plans to feed your friendships!

	Activity	Time	Place
My friend(s)			
Your friend(s)			
Our friends			
New friends			

∞48∞
Forgiveness and Acceptance

*It's really not forgiveness
In marriage that's divine,
But remembering to forget:
That's when love is blind.*

The Exercise Goal

To identify any areas of unforgiveness in our marriage and offer the gift of forgiveness to each other.

The Biblical Idea

"To err is human; to forgive is divine." Have you ever wondered why forgiveness is considered divine? Perhaps it is because only someone like God can forgive unconditionally. We may forgive, but we like to remind those who hurt us that we still remember.

Not Joseph. Thrown into an animal pit by his brothers, sold into slavery, accused wrongly of sexual assault by Potiphar's wife, and imprisoned and forgotten for two years, Joseph nevertheless chose to forgive his offenders. When his brothers stood trembling before him years later, Joseph offered them the gift of forgiveness. He refused to hold them accountable for their wrongdoing.

That's the kind of gift Hosea gave to his unfaithful wife Gomer when he ransomed her from the auction block of shame. That's what Jesus did for the thief on the cross when Jesus said, "Today, you will be with me in paradise." That's what he did for you and me by offering his life as a payment for our offenses. And that's the kind of gift we owe our mates: unconditional, unrestrained, and undeserved forgiveness.

God said, "I will remember their sins no more" (Jer. 31:34). *Remember* comes from the root word "to mark or to record, to make mention of." God still knows what we've done, but he makes mention of it no more. He does not record it to our account. Jesus wiped the slate clean.

There is never a sin too great, never a hurt too deep, never a word too harsh, never an act too degrading for Jesus to forgive. In our ignorance we sin against him, but Jesus' words, like a brilliant rainbow after a destructive flood, give us hope: "Father, forgive them, for they know not what they do" (Luke 23:34 KJV).

The Need

We have a bathroom sink that's constantly getting clogged. Each time I (Becky) pull out the drain plug, I find the culprit: a gooey mass of hair and other assorted goodies that have plugged the pipe. Water can't drain freely until I pull that stuff out.

That's the way it is with marriage. Tangled masses of unwanted trash fill our lives daily: unkind words, selfish actions, mixed-up priorities, or harbored resentments. Mutual confession, understanding, and forgiveness flush the drainpipes in marriage and allow love to flow smoothly and sweetly again.

Forgiveness truly is a gift you give your mate. It doesn't eliminate any recurring negative feelings, but forgiveness is a process that ultimately will change your thoughts and feelings about your mate to those of deeper love and acceptance. Advice columnist Ann Landers once wrote, "Forgiveness is setting the prisoner free and then discovering you were the prisoner." Love is being willing to say not only, "I'm sorry; I was wrong," but also, "I forgive you." It's cheaper than calling the plumber.

The Exercise

Are there any clogged drains in your marriage? Work on these exercises, then share with your mate.

1. A time when I felt truly forgiven.
2. Something for which I need to forgive myself.
3. Something for which I need to ask your forgiveness.

The Plan

Search your heart for any areas of unforgiveness toward your mate. List them, then cross them out as you forgive. Do this whenever you sense you are harboring anger and unforgiveness toward your mate. Pray about each area.

∽ 49 ∽
Attitudes

Lord, make our thoughts beautiful,
Resting on what is true;
For an attitude of gratitude
Is what we owe to you.

The Exercise Goal

To develop healthy, affirmative attitudes about life and our marriage.

The Biblical Idea

What we think about greatly influences our outlook on life. Philippians 4:8 suggests several things to consider: whatever is true, noble, right, pure, lovely, admirable, excellent, or praiseworthy. Paul knew that the secret of contentment lies not only in being happy with our circumstances, but also in making intentional thought choices.

Can you imagine your every thought being flashed on a public screen? Jesus knew the thoughts of people before they ever spoke. Remember the Pharisees? Jesus openly rebuked them for their thinking: "You blind guides!" he said. "You strain out a gnat but swallow a camel. . . . You clean the outside of the cup and dish, but inside they are full of greed and self-indulgence" (Matt. 23:24–25). Their negative outlook and concentration on rules and laws blinded them from the real truth and from the positive hope Jesus offered.

To form good attitudes we need good models. Paul said, "Your attitude should be the same as that of Christ Jesus" (Phil. 2:5). Jesus knew his identity and purpose on earth. And he focused constantly on his Father. Is it any wonder he mirrored humility, truth, love, hope, and perfection?

149

Attitudes, both positive and negative, are formed early in life. We watch. We listen. We observe the significant people in our lives and frequently copy the attitudes we see and hear. But we need not remain prisoners of those thoughts. Instead, we are to capture and imprison every thought (2 Cor. 10:5). We all bear a personal responsibility and choice.

The Need

"That's just the way I am!" "You're never going to change!" "Nothing good ever happens to us!" Fatalist attitudes like that will kill a marriage. We have known couples who just couldn't seem to release each other from their past actions. Still focusing on the hurt of an affair, verbal abuse, foolish money management, or dishonesty, they refused to abandon their problems.

Two things that may help us focus positively on our marriage are to visualize how we really want our marriage to be and how we can be active participants in that vision. Painting an ideal picture is not a denial of reality. It is focusing on a goal. It is the carrot dangled before the reluctant donkey, spurring it to move ahead. The carrot—the reward—is the eventual reality of changed attitudes, affirmative responses, and greater marriage intimacy.

Meditating on Scripture keeps us focused positively. And if your memory is fading, bring out that journal. There are times when I (Becky) choose to record only the profitable events of the day, the good characteristics in my mate or myself, the blessings God is giving. Like praise prayers to God, those affirmative thoughts crowd out the negativism in our lives and usher in his power.

The Exercise

What consumes your thoughts during the day? Are you a winner or a whiner? Do you smell roses or burnt coffee? Think about how you've formed your attitudes, complete these questions, then share your answers together.

1. Three good things about myself.

2. Three good things about our marriage.

3. Three ways I'd like to improve my general attitude.

The Plan

List three ways you can help each other maintain a positive, healthy outlook on your marriage, life, and yourself.

1.

2.

3.

∽ *50* ∽
Needs

Time together? Time apart?
Close communion, heart-to-heart?
Love, respect, and balance, too:
What needs I can, I'll meet for you.

The Exercise Goal

To understand and work toward satisfying each other's needs.

The Biblical Idea

God designed both partners with different needs. Ephesians 5 suggests some of the needs of a man: respect, fellowship, and admiration as a leader and a man. A woman craves love, security, understanding, and an appreciation for herself as a person. As husbands and wives, we can help meet some of those needs for each other, but no mate is equipped to meet all of them.

At times, even couples in the Bible failed to satisfy each other. At one point, Sarah followed her husband's wishes and ended up in Pharaoh's harem. God intervened and sent diseases to Pharaoh's family as a warning not to touch Sarah (Gen. 12). If Abraham had respected his wife's need for security, he would not have told a half-truth and placed Sarah in such a dangerous predicament. And if Sarah had believed in Abraham's leadership as a man, perhaps she would not have chosen a surrogate mother before Isaac was born (Gen. 16).

"Be sure you know the condition of your flocks," says Proverbs 27:23. The Good Shepherd not only knows his sheep's condition, but also he anticipates and provides for their needs. Still waters, refreshing moments, good food, joyful paths, protection from the enemy—he provides it all. We will not want, as long as we follow his leading.

Therefore, in marriage God's desire is for husbands and wives to trust him for all their needs, being content with the mate he gave them. Why, then, would we look for greener pastures?

The Need

In the earlier years of our marriage, we had a "Read my mind!" philosophy. We assumed the other person had some kind of sixth sense to discern our deepest desires. Without realizing it, we were storing up ammunition for an emotional showdown in the future.

Later, as we began to work through some issues in our marriage, we discovered each had needs the other could not completely fulfill. We began to concentrate on those we could help meet, then acknowledged that only God could supply the rest.

Becky had always felt selfish expressing a need. We worked through that barrier and began listing our needs. We presented our lists to each other, examining how we could break the needs down into reachable goals that would help the other person meet the need. Our lists included: "I need to know you love me in little ways"; "I need to know you appreciate what I do"; "I need space as well as time together"; and "I need a certain amount of organization in my life."

But even with our lists, frequent verbal reminders from each other, such as, "Do you feel I'm meeting your needs in this area?" kept us accountable. Like Hannah Whitall Smith suggests, "Mind the checks."[11] Stay sensitive to the nudging of the Holy Spirit.

The Exercise

Work on your individual lists. Then share them together.

1. My needs—emotional, physical, and spiritual.

2. Three needs you've met for me in the past and how you've met them.

3. Three ways you can help satisfy my needs in the future.

The Plan

Discuss your needs. Decide what needs you can meet in each other and which you will have to trust God to satisfy. List three of your mate's needs that you can meet and describe how you will meet them.

1. My mate's need _____

   How I can meet it _____

2. My mate's need _____

   How I can meet it _____

3. My mate's need _____

   How I can meet it _____

∽ *51* ∽
Change

We may sag around the middle
And our temples may turn gray;
But let's keep our love growing,
Whatever comes our way.

The Exercise Goal

To give emotional support to each other through times of change.

The Biblical Idea

The crunching of brittle, golden leaves; the crackling of a warm, winter fire; the fragrance of sweet, velvet roses; and the taste of cold lemonade on a hot summer's day: There's nothing like experiencing the pleasures unique to each season. God created the seasons almost as a picture of life itself: "As long as the earth endures, seedtime and harvest, cold and heat, summer and winter, day and night will never cease" (Gen. 8:22).

Winter comes, a ruthless killer of all life. Yet when the fragrance of springtime emerges, every new bud cries out, "Resurrection!" "Beauty!" "Hope!" "There's life after death!" Summer brings a rest, a pause in nature's busy production schedule. Fall offers a harvest of reflection at the growth and change that has evolved through the years.

All of nature needs change. The seed planted, yet dying in the ground, bursts forth in the radically new form of a beautiful flower. The butterfly struggles out of its silky cocoon. The eagle nudges its young out of the nest, swooping down to catch them until they can soar by themselves. Animals grow new coats, sufficient for warmth during the chilling months of hibernation. And we humans shed our outgrown habits, plant new seeds, bury old dreams, and reap fresh harvests of joy. There can be no growth without change.

"Consider it pure joy," says James, "whenever you face trials of many kinds" (James 1:2). Often change comes to us in the form of trials and adversity. Problems—and change—are opportunities for joy!

The Need

If change is so important for growth, why do we fear it in marriage? We like our cocoons. Our nests are warm and comfortable. What if we fall? What if we tire of the struggle and end up a crippled moth?

Dr. Frank Minirth of Minirth-Meier Clinic says this about the changes from the twenties to midlife:

> Young love is great. Your twenties were great as you firmed up your commitments, laid out goals. You decided how your own family would run. The thirties are tremendously productive, high-energy years. Then the forties. You can't see as well, your parents are starting to die, you yourself are slowing down physically. . . . Midlife is tough. In my opinion, maybe one of the worst phases.[12]

Midlife is one of the most difficult periods of change a married couple faces. These are the years that yield so many sexual affairs, affairs usually begun because the people having them can't handle the pressures associated with change. However, Dr. Minirth and the other authors of *Passages of Marriage*, quickly add that this is a time when love often renews itself, when couples can draw even closer together.

What changes are you going through? Young marrieds, still simmering in the flames of romance, suddenly face parenthood. Even if the new infant is "planned," that third party can threaten the intimacy of their marriage union. Parents whose otherwise sane and gentle children come unraveled in adolescence find a new challenge in change. Bulging waistlines, bifocals, and graying hair may mark the passage into midlife and a fresh, new identity crisis. And as children leave the nest, Mom and Dad may stare at each other with a "Now-what-do-we-do?" look.

Illness, job changes, and death bring unexpected change that threatens a couple's marital stability. At times, circumstances may force couples to make a mid-course correction in their journey and require outside help to survive the trauma. But those who can support each other with gentle love, thoughtful affirmations, and positive choices will find their changes becoming stepping-stones toward a closer bond. And when the butterfly emerges, you'll know the struggle was worthwhile.

The Exercise

Think about the changes you and your mate have faced in the past and recently, even those yet to come. Answer the following questions and then discuss them together.

1. Three changes we've experienced since we married.

2. Three ways we've grown as a result of those changes.

3. A change (changes) that is (are) difficult for me right now.

4. Three ways you can help me get through these changes.

The Plan

Think of three ways in general that you can help each other in times of change.

1.

2.

3.

∞ *52* ∞
Fears

Hiding deep inside are things
I've never let you see.
If I share my heart with you,
Will you love the real me?

The Exercise Goal

To become closer to each other by disclosing any hidden fears to each other.

The Biblical Idea

The knees knock together, the throat feels parched, the muscles tense up, and every organ in the body suddenly responds with a red alert. You know the feeling, don't you? Fear grips all of us at one time or another.

Fear does strange things. It made Adam and Eve don fig leaves and hunt for a hiding place from God. It turned Elijah, a mighty prophet of God, into the coward of Judah county. Fear drove Gideon into a winepress to thresh wheat—away from the eyes of the Midianite terrorists. Fear paralyzes; disclosure heals. Fear imprisons; disclosure frees. The psalmist expresses best what God desires for couples: "Surely you desire truth in the inner parts" (Ps. 51:6). When we disclose our deepest fears to our mates, we are sharing truth from our inner parts.

The Need

In John Powell's book *Why Am I Afraid to Tell You Who I Am?* he challenges us to analyze the reasons behind our fears. Afraid of rejection, abandonment, embarrassment, isolation, or failure, we often maintain "fronts" to disguise our inner fears. False beliefs such as

"If you really knew what I was like or what I did, you wouldn't love me" can cut off all roads to a closer relationship. Real intimacy comes when we are willing to stand before our mates with hearts and souls exposed.

What about the risk? Husbands who are afraid to admit their job or parental insecurities, wives who are unable to communicate their fears of mothering, aging, or loneliness, even Christians who are afraid to be perceived as faithless doubters—all pretend nothing is wrong and never peel away the layers to expose the heart hungers they feel. "I must be in control," "I must be strong," or "I must be perfect" are thought patterns that bring only depression and destruction. God has given husbands and wives, more than any other people, the privilege of sharing on a deeper level. The pain of disclosure is never as great as the pain of isolation.

The Exercise

What are your fears? The dark? Heights? Crowds? Do you freeze at the thought of true intimacy, especially if it means unveiling your past failures? Think about your fears, your secrets, any areas in your life that you've hidden from your mate. Then answer the following questions and plan a time to share your answers together.

1. Three of my biggest fears.

2. Something I've never told you about myself.

The Plan

Three ways you can help alleviate each other's fears and give each other a safe place to share them.

1.

2.

3.

∽Notes∾

1. Robert Hall, *The Encyclopedia of Religious Quotations*, ed. and comp. Frank S. Mead (Westwood, N.J.: Fleming H. Revell, 1965), 340.

2. Ronald Dunn, "Teach Us to Pray," *Today's Better Life*, Winter 1993, 110.

3. Charles R. Swindoll, *Growing Wise in Family Life* (Portland, Oreg.: Multnomah Press, 1988), 40.

4. Dale Hanson Bourke, "Surprised by Grace," *Today's Better Life*, Winter 1993, 37.

5. Kip and Kristine Barkley, "Real People, Real Voices: Play Mates," *Marriage*, November/December 1993, 52.

6. Richard A. Swenson, M.D., *Margin: How to Create the Emotional, Physical, Financial & Time Reserves You Need* (Colorado Springs: NavPress Publishing Group, 1992), 154–55.

7. Gerald Foley, "If You Really Love Me—Then Fight!" in *Courage to Love When Your Marriage Hurts* (Notre Dame: Ave Maria Press, 1992). Reprinted from *Marriage*, November/December 1993, 17.

8. Frank and Mary Alice Minirth, Brian and Deborah Newman, Robert and Susan Hemfelt, *Passages of Marriage* (Nashville: Thomas Nelson Publishers, 1991), 19.

9. Bruce Wilkinson, *The 7 Laws of the Learner*, Teacher's Notebook (Atlanta: Walk Thru the Bible Ministries, Inc., 1988), 119.

10. Swenson, *Margin*, 152.

11. Hannah Whitall Smith, *The Christian's Secret of a Happy Life* (Uhrichsville, Ohio: Barbour and Company, Inc., 1985), 101.

12. Frank Minirth, *Passages of Marriage*, 161–62.

Because God has given us a deep desire to strengthen marriages, we are committed to sharing with other couples preventive maintenance to take care of their marriages, and food for thought that can enrich them. If this book helps you, please let us know. We are also available to lead marriage enrichment events for your group or your church. You can write to us in care of the publisher.